TOM CHATFIELD is a writer and commentator. The author of
three previous books exploring digital culture, he has worked
with companies including Google and Mind Candy, and spoken
at forums including TED Global and the World IT Congress.
A fortnightly columnist for the BBC, he also writes fiction and
plays jazz piano. For more, see tomchatfield.net

THE SCHOOL OF LIFE is dedicated to exploring life's big questions:
*How can we fulfil our potential? Can work be inspiring? Why does
community matter? Can relationships last a lifetime?* We don't have all
the answers, but we will direct you towards a variety of useful ideas
– from philosophy to literature, psychology to the visual arts – that
are guaranteed to stimulate, provoke, nourish and console.

How to Thrive
in the Digital Age
Tom Chatfield

MACMILLAN

First published 2012 by Macmillan
an imprint of Pan Macmillan, a division
of Macmillan Publishers Limited

Pan Macmillan
20 New Wharf Road, London N1 9RR
Basingstoke and Oxford
Associated companies throughout the world
www.panmacmillan.com

ISBN 978-1-4472-0231-8

Copyright © The School of Life 2012

The right of Tom Chatfield to be identified
as the author of this work has been asserted
by him in accordance with the Copyright,
Designs and Patents Act 1988.

The picture and text acknowledgements
on page 150 constitute an extension of this
copyright page.

Every effort has been made to contact the
copyright holders of the material reproduced
in this book. If any have been inadvertently
overlooked, the publisher will be pleased to
make restitution at the earliest opportunity.

9 8 7 6 5 4 3 2 1

A CIP catalogue record for this book is
available from the British Library.

Cover designed by Marcia Mihotich
Text design and setting by seagulls.net
Printed and bound by CPI Group (UK) Ltd,
Croydon, CR0 4YY

Visit www.panmacmillan.com to read
more about all our books and to buy
them. You will also find features,
author interviews and news of any
author events, and you can sign up for
e-newsletters so that you're always first
to hear about our new releases.

I went to the woods because I wished to live deliberately, to front only the essential facts of life, and see if I could not learn what it had to teach, and not, when I came to die, discover that I had not lived. I did not wish to live what was not life, living is so dear; nor did I wish to practise resignation, unless it was quite necessary. I wanted to live deep and suck out all the marrow of life . . .
– Henry David Thoreau, *Walden*

Contents

Introduction   I

1. From Past to Present   9

2. Wired and Unwired Time   23

3. Taking Control   37

4. Reframing Technology   53

5. Sharing, Expertise and the End of Authority   67

6. On Becoming Less than Human   85

7. Play and Pleasure   IOI

8. The New Politics   II7

Conclusion   I3I

Homework   I4I

Introduction

We live in an age of miracles so commonplace that it can be difficult to see them as anything other than part of the daily texture of living. This is the technology writer and theorist Kevin Kelly, blogging in August 2011:

> I've had to persuade myself to believe in the impossible more often . . . Twenty years ago if I had been paid to convince an audience of reasonable, educated people that in twenty years time we'd have street and satellite maps for the entire world on our personal hand held phone devices – for free – and with street views for many cities – I would not be able to do it. I could not have made an economic case for how this could come about 'for free'. It was starkly impossible back then.

The impossible facts of our age are only just beginning. Ahead of us lie new forms of collaboration and interaction whose outlines we are, perhaps, beginning to glimpse in the fact that the internet-connected phones increasingly found in every pocket are more powerful than most computers were ten years ago. In another decade's time, billions of people will have at their fingertips the kind of resources that only governments commanded twenty years ago.

The pace of these changes is another unprecedented thing. Television and radio have been with us for over a century; print for more than 500 years. Yet in just two decades, we have moved from the public opening-up of the internet to its connection to more than two billion people; and it has been just three decades between the launch of the first commercial cellular-phone system and the connection of more than five billion active accounts.

This smart global network is likely, in the future, to connect not only us, but many of the objects in our lives – from cars and clothes to food and drink. Through smart chips and centralized databases, we are gaining an unprecedented kind of connection not only to each other, but to the manufactured world around us: its tools, its shared spaces, its patterns of action and reaction. And with all of this comes new information about the world, in new kinds of quantities: information about where we are, what we are doing, and what we are like.

What are we to make of this information? And, equally importantly, what is already being made of it by others – by governments; by corporations; by activists, criminals, law-enforcers and creators? Knowledge and power have always been closely entwined. Today, though, information and the infrastructure through which it flows represent not only power, but a new kind of economic and social force.

Intellectually, socially and legislatively, we are lagging years, if not decades, behind the facts of the present. Generationally, the divide between those 'natives' born into a digital era and those who grew up before it can seem a chasm across which common understandings and shared values are difficult to articulate.

This book examines the question of what it may mean for all of us not simply to exist but to thrive within a digital world; to 'live deep', in

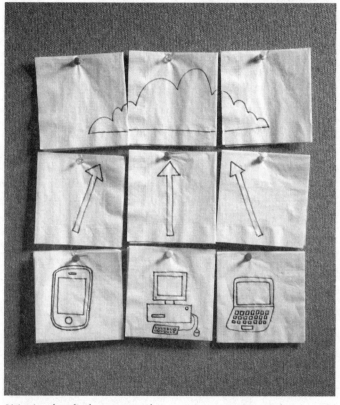

Living in a data cloud: smart networks are starting to connect not only us, but everything from cars to clothing.

Thoreau's phrase, and to make the most of the unfolding possibilities of our times.

Exploring these possibilities is like exploring a new city or continent. We are entering a place where human nature remains the same, but the structures shaping it are alien. Today's digital world is not simply an idea or a set of tools, any more than a modern digital device is simply something switched on for leisure or pleasure. Rather, for an ever-increasing number of people, it is a gateway to the place where leisure and labour alike are rooted: an arena within which we seamlessly juggle friendships, media, business, shopping, research, politics, play, finance, and much else besides.

When it comes to the question of thriving, my aim is to trace two interwoven stories: first, how we as individuals can thrive in the digital world; and second, how society can help us both to realize our potential in this world, and to relate to others in as fully human a way as possible.

These stories both begin in the same place, with the history of digital machines. I then go on to explore one of the most central questions of the present state of technology: what it means to be able to say 'no' as well as 'yes' to the tools in our lives, and to make the best of ourselves both by using technology and by deliberately carving out time for *not* using it.

I'll also talk about those challenges that almost all of us – whether we know it or not – grapple with every day: issues of personal identity, privacy, communication, attention, and the regulation of all the above. If there is a common thread here, it is the question of how individual experience fits into the new kind of collective life of the twenty-first century: how what 'I' am relates to what others know of me, what I share with those others, and what can remain personal and private.

The second half of this book examines the cultural and political structures encompassing these interests, and what the 'contracts' of decent digital citizenship might look like. Finally, I'll return to that most central of questions: what it means to live well in an age that holds unparalleled opportunities both for narcissism and for connection to others.

The nature of digital technology is as protean as our own, and can play many parts in our lives: facilitator, library, friend, seducer, comfort, prison. Ultimately, though, all of its shifting screens are also mirrors, in which we have the opportunity to see ourselves and each other as never before. Or, of course, we can look away.

1. From Past to Present

I.

The brief story of human interactions with digital technologies has been one of steadily increasing intimacy: of the integration, within half a century, of a startlingly new kind of tool into the heart of billions of lives.

The first electronic digital computers, developed in the 1940s, were vast and dauntingly complex machines, devised and operated by some of the world's finest minds: pioneers like Alan Turing, whose theoretical and practical work helped the British to decode encrypted German messages during the Second World War.

The next generation of computers, mainframes, arose in the late 1950s. Existing largely within academic and military institutions, mainframes still occupied entire rooms and were also the province of specialists – their inputs taking the form of highly abstracted commands, their outputs meaningless to anyone not versed in computer science.

All this began to change in the 1970s, with the rise of the microprocessor and the arrival of the first computers in ordinary homes rather than laboratories. Thomas Watson, the president of IBM, is famously reported to have said in 1943. 'I think there is a world market for maybe five computers.' Whether he made this claim or not (no less an authority than Wikipedia declares there's 'scant evidence' that he did), when the world's first personal computer was released as a kit in 1971, nobody expected the domestic market for such machines to run far beyond a few thousand enthusiasts.

Computing, however, proved an attraction far beyond anything the most ambitious academics had conceived. By the end of the 1970s, new machines by Apple, Commodore and Tandy were selling hundreds of thousands of units. The digital revolution had gone public.

Even this was only the beginning of the steady integration of human–digital interactions. Since the 1970s, our machines have grown ever more powerful, more interconnected and easier to use. Those we use today are hundreds of thousands of times more powerful than the first domestic generation, tens of times cheaper, and immeasurably easier to use.

More important than power, however, is the *experience* that these machines provide. In this, the great revolution is only just beginning. Because personal computing, in the sense of a desktop computer at home or a laptop carried in a bag, is steadily being replaced by something else: the smartphone in the hand or the tablet on the table, switched on and networked at all times.

We are, I believe, steadily moving from merely personal computing towards what might be called 'intimate computing', representing a whole new level of integration between digital technologies and life. In coffee shops and living rooms, personal digital devices are handled with a solicitude and frequency that might once have been reserved for a partner or favourite pet. For a generation of so-called digital natives, a mobile phone is often the first thing you touch when you wake up in the morning and the last thing you touch when you go to bed at night.

2.

All technologies change us as we use them: 'we shape our tools, and thereafter our tools shape us' as the Canadian pioneer of media studies Marshall McLuhan put it. In releasing us from reliance on daily hunting-and-gathering, technologies, from early agriculture to refrigeration, have helped us build cities and civilizations. In changing our mobility, transportation technologies have shifted our relationships with time and space. We are technological creatures. It is in our natures to augment ourselves and our world – to exceed and adapt.

Since the invention of writing more than five millennia ago, the world has been transformed by what the American sociologist Daniel Bell called 'intellectual technologies': technologies that allow us to extend our minds in much the same way as weapons and clothing extend the power of our bodies. From maps to movies, we build tools that enhance our appreciation of the world and our capacities for learning and communication, and allow us to pass on our knowledge and inspirations.

Even among such technologies, digital computers are unique. As Alan Turing foresaw in the 1930s, in his envisioning of a Universal Turing Machine able to compute every single function it is possible to solve, computers are the first truly universal medium: mechanisms of an almost limitless flexibility.

From words to images to film, a computer is able to simulate all other media. With the correct software installed, it can reproduce sounds, video, images and text at will – and can send and receive these for the merest fraction of the cost and the time such operations

Thanks to intellectual technologies like writing, we've been augmenting our minds for millennia.

have historically taken. For the first time in history, all our media and communications needs – indeed, all the intellectual technologies in our lives – can be provided via a single, integrated system.

I can still go to the cinema to watch films, if I wish, just as I can flick through television channels, pick up physical books, or listen to music through my CD player. In every case, though, these acts are no longer strictly necessary. Because I own an internet-connected digital device, a whole universe of sounds, words and images lies at my fingertips. Whether I'm at home or on the move, I can access everything from the latest *CSI: Miami* episode to *Moby Dick*, or endless home videos of cats. And I can also access interactive services, from games to online shopping, that no other medium has ever provided.

Through technology, then, we are all in control as we have never been before. And underpinning this control lie the weightless, infinitely reproducible structures of information itself: the ones and zeroes of electrical charge, from which the possibilities of this word 'digital' ultimately flow.

Throughout history, the power of mind-enhancing technologies has always been limited by the physical stuff of reality. Until the invention of printing, producing a book was a labour that demanded hundreds of hours of expert craftsmanship. Even with the printing press, the physical bulk and expense of paper restricted what could be done with written words. Recorded sounds were, for the first century of their existence, limited by what could physically be etched into a substance like wax or vinyl. Cinema and photography relied on expensive, limited physical materials – delicate, flammable reels of carefully prepared film.

Inner space: there are now more pages on the web than there are stars in our galaxy.

All of this has now been swept away. At the time of writing, in late 2011, an estimated one hour of video footage is uploaded to the web for every one minute of real time that passes. We have grown accustomed to the idea of information suffusion. Behind our resignation to the fact that there's more out there than we can ever consume, however, lies a still-steepening curve, with the world's sum total of digital information continuing to grow at an exponential rate.

By 2008, there were an estimated one trillion pages on the World Wide Web. Three years later, it makes little sense even to estimate the number, but it runs to many trillions. Around a hundred billion books have been published in the half-millennium since the invention of printing, if every language and edition is taken into account. That volume of information represents less than a month's worth of the content currently being uploaded to the net.

Most important of all is the fact that digital devices are able not only to display and to reproduce information: they also have the capacity to *animate* it, breathing life into bytes and algorithms. When we program a computer, we are not simply creating an object as we do if we are writing a book, painting a picture or drawing a map. We are setting a system in motion for others to interact with and explore. We are building other worlds.

This is perhaps the central miracle of our age – and the one that best explains the continuing migration of human effort, attention, emotion, economic activity and innovation towards digital technologies. Just as cities have acted as magnets for much of the world's population over the past few hundred years, the digital realm is drawing people into its dense possibilities: into simulations that speak to us more deeply than many merely real experiences.

3.

If we are interested in living with technology in the best possible way, we must recognize that what matters above all is not the individual devices we use, but what we use them *for*. Digital media are technologies of the mind and of experience. If we wish to thrive in their company, the first lesson is that we can only hope constructively to comprehend them if we speak not of technology in the abstract, but of the experiences it enables.

Consider the routine of my own digital experiences. On an average day, I send and receive a couple of text messages, read and send twenty to thirty emails, Tweet a handful of times, and log between two and twelve hours at the screen of a computer, reading and writing and interacting online.

As I type this, I'm probably asking the same question as you are, reading it: where do those two to twelve hours go? I can account for bits and pieces of them, most easily in the form of word counts for articles and books. Yet the honest answer is not only that I don't know, but that it would make little sense to tot up that activity under segments with titles like 'social networking' or 'blogging' or 'online gaming'. To do so would be like accounting for my reading habits by saying I spend two hours a day 'turning over pages'. In each case, the significance of the experience lies elsewhere.

When I'm reading a physical book, knowing what I'm reading and for how long will tell you a lot about the nature of my experience. Even though I have to determine what a book means to *me*, I'm reading the same book as everyone else, and I'm probably doing so in the same way: from start to finish. I'm not simply creating an entirely new book as I go along, in any order that pleases me – which is exactly what happens when I use a service like Facebook.

What's more, when I'm using Facebook, I'm not acting alone. I'm entering a kind of public space, and responding from minute to minute to the people and objects I find around me. I might update my status, follow a few friends' links, then find myself drawn into a discussion around a book or film, or debating the merits of a night out. I'll almost certainly follow dozens of links elsewhere, and read these while browsing a handful of other sites, checking email, and listening to some music or talk radio.

Reporting, after an hour of this, that I've been 'using Facebook' sheds little light on either the nature or the quality of my experiences. What's needed is something that engages with the kind of encounters and interactions I've had: a measure of my feelings and motivations, and a recognition that the reality of these is not diminished by the unreality of the arena I've been acting within. I will almost certainly have shared news and views with dozens of other people in an hour online – and how I feel about what's happened is likely to colour my impressions of the rest of the day.

This is not to say that I'm the same person online as I am in the flesh. However, the best criteria for judging my experience are precisely those that I would apply to most other social experiences and interactions in my life: how much I managed to learn or to communicate; how emotionally connected I felt to others; how enriched the rest of my life was by my interactions.

Some rewards are easier to find digitally than others. Getting what we want online is often distant from getting what we need – although both tend to happen faster. Disembodied, moving through online space, we are afforded greater ease than when we are sharing a physical environment. We are able more easily both to be altruistic and open, and to deceive and cause grief – our lives made easier by ignoring the human realities beyond each screen.

Technology is, in this sense, a kind of amplifier applied to our natures – a realm of possibilities that, at its worse, risks reducing other people to the level of objects: presences that we turn on or off at will, and to which we owe little respect or honesty. Veiled behind ever greater complexities, we perpetually risk distancing ourselves from fully committed relationships with each other, and from fully introspective relationships with ourselves.

Yet the evidence of the last three decades of online activity is not solely of objectification or facile self-delight. When I look at the digital landscape in 2011, I see an arena desperate to extract greater depth from its public spaces – to personalize and to humanize at all costs. How else to explain our willingness to make the digital aspects of our lives ever more complex and messily human?

4.

It is individual human bonds and serendipities that matter most online; and it is these above all that will mould technology's future. A world in which every living person has the technological fluency of today's youngest generation is still hard to imagine. But it will be one in which distances of all kinds have a very different significance to today – and in which families and friends, young and old, interact far more freely and frequently across geographical and generational divides.

In many ways, it is the elderly, the socially disadvantaged and others who have traditionally been excluded who stand to gain most from the rise and rise of new technologies: grandparents who might otherwise barely have a chance to know their grandchildren; those in the developing world for whom contact with family, friends and peers elsewhere may make a transforming difference to their quality of life, or who have long been isolated by poor infrastructure, poverty and political restrictions.

Above all, today's digital realm is being swelled by the human experiences and values flowing into it. Over three-quarters of a billion people have freely uploaded much of their most intimate selves to Facebook alone in the half-decade since its public launch. Avatars and second selves in games and other social sites offer not just an escape from actuality, but a path towards other people and towards new kinds of connection. Rumours, lies and hatreds abound online – but so too do remarkable new forms of trust, from the billions of strangers who trade goods on eBay to services like Alibaba.com, which allows more than sixty million people involved in small businesses to match each others' skills and needs.

It is a dizzying maelstrom – and a profoundly disturbing one at times. Yet it is still *us*, in all of our humanity, entering these new spaces and having these experiences. And it is only by speaking of these experiences in the long-established humanist vocabulary of feelings, ideas and values that we can best hope to 'live deep' in present times – and to understand a future in which technology will ever more intimately mediate and define what it means to be human.

2. Wired and Unwired Time

I.

The August 1921 edition of the American magazine *The Wireless Age* devoted eleven pages to a breathless account of the boxing 'battle of the century'. This was the world heavyweight title fight that took place the previous month in Jersey City, in which the American brawler Jack 'The Manassa Mauler' Dempsey knocked out the French challenger Georges Carpentier in the fourth round.

It was a grand day for sport, with over a million dollars in ticket sales taken at the doors. But this wasn't the reason *The Wireless Age* lavished so much attention on the event. The second of July 1921 was also a historic day in the brief history of broadcasting. For this was the first time that the live mediated audience for a major event had outnumbered those watching in person. Ninety thousand had packed the Jersey City arena. But, by the magazine's estimation, 'a multitude – not less than 300,000 persons – tense and eager' had followed the fight from afar.

They had done so thanks to what was essentially a telephone attached by a long wire to one of the largest wireless aerials yet built: an antenna 680 feet long suspended above the Erie-Lackawanna Railroad Terminal at Hoboken in New Jersey. Its wire ran all the way to the excitable person of J. Andrew White, who, as acting president of the National Amateur Wireless Association, described events

Thanks to the Amateur Wireless Association, Dempsey vs. Carpentier in August 1921 provided a tipping point in the history of media.

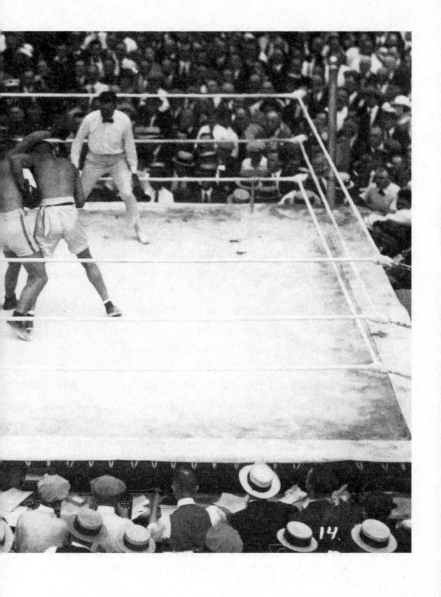

from the ringside. In accordance with a last-minute change in plan, *The Wireless Age* somewhat sheepishly noted, White's words were repeated by a second operator at the terminal, and it was his voice that rode the airwaves.

The magazine was fully aware of the power of the precedent being set, calling the broadcast 'A record . . . and the ushering in of a new era. For while the eyes of the world were awaiting the issuance of the time-honoured descriptive printed word to tell the story – radio told it by voice! Instantly, through the ears of an expectant public, a world event had been "pictured" in all its thrilling details . . . . The appeal to the imagination is boundless. Forecasts for the future now can be made a subject for pleasant, stimulating and practically endless speculation.'

Less than a century later, it's safe to say that even the wildest of these speculations have been exceeded. Over two billion people are now connected to the internet, and more than double that number are connected to each other via mobile phones. Live audiences for news and sporting events regularly run into the hundreds of millions. Over half the people alive today are almost permanently accessible to the world via some form of 'live' digital connection.

These are numbers to gawp at. What has gone almost unnoticed compared to these shifts, however, is that we have over the first decade of the present century begun to pass through another wired watershed: one to do not with raw numbers, but with time itself.

In 1999, according to a survey of over two thousand Americans aged between 8 and 18 conducted by the Kaiser Family Foundation, this age group were using media for around six hours and twenty minutes each day. Young people's lives, it noted, were close to 'saturation' – that is, those analysing the survey's results could see almost no room for more time to be spent using media.

Humanity, it seemed, was reaching an inexorable plateau in the amount of media it was possible to consume within the waking hours of a day – a conclusion supported by an aggregate increase of just two minutes in daily media consumption among the same age group when the same survey was repeated in 2004.

The Foundation conducted the same survey once again, however, in 2009, and to its surprise found that the total daily media usage of eight-to-eighteen-year-olds had now increased by over 20 per cent, to almost seven hours and forty minutes. If the use of multiple devices was included, total media exposure rose to around ten hours and forty-five minutes daily.

This was an astonishing result. Given that young people need between eight and nine hours of sleep a night, the 2009 figures pushed media usage past half of all waking hours – even without including any media used for work at school rather than leisure. Television still dominated, as it has done for half a century, with over three hours and forty minutes daily. But by far the most important recent trend was the use of devices like iPhones to consume old and new media alike: to watch downloaded television shows on the bus to school; to send text messages and check Facebook while listening to music and checking emails.

Within just half a decade, media had moved from saturating leisure time at home to something still more significant: not so much the saturation of daily life as a complete integration into its routines and activities. As a similar report into media habits published in November 2010 by the POLIS initiative in London concluded, most young people in the developed world are now never without access to the protective media bubbles created by devices like smartphones and tablets. A portable, personal supply of songs, videos, games, applications and social-media services is permanently on tap.

Behavioural norms are being disrupted at a pace even the rise of radio broadcasting in the 1920s and television in the 1950s did not match. And the most important development of all, for me, is how this change relates to a different kind of norm: not just our habits, but what we consider to be our default 'waking state'.

Today, for the first time in history, it's true to say that many people's daily default is to be 'wired' into at least one personalized form of media. Where less than a century ago the live wire of the radio broadcast was considered close to a miracle, it is now common-place for the majority of our conscious hours to be spent plugged into our very own live link to the world.

The most obvious question that follows is a pragmatic one: what happens next? In the short term, the answer is likely to be still more media use, at more times and in more places. If we are to thrive in the long term, though, I believe that these trends mean we must start thinking in a new way about the different kinds of time in our lives.

Time away from digital media is not only no longer our default state; it is also something we cannot experience without explicitly aiming to do so. Consider the 'quiet carriage' signs found in most trains, or those signs in museums, restaurants and other public spaces requesting that people turn off their mobile phones. These are signs of our times in the literal sense: indications that the absence of digital devices has to be specially requested.

If we are to get the most out of both the world around us and each other, we need to recognize that we now have two fundamentally different ways of being in the world: our wired and our unwired states. Simply deploring one or the other helps nobody, for each represents a different set of possibilities for thought and action. Rather, we must learn to ask – and teach our children to ask – which aspects of a task, and of living, are best served by each. And we must find ways of effectively building each into our way of life.

2.

The greatest advantages of wired living are easily enumerated. Plugged into the world's hive-mind, we have speed, we have range; we can research and reference much of humanity's gathered knowledge – and gossip and opinion – in a matter of minutes; we are mere moments away from contact with thousands of others. We have godlike capabilities, and are increasingly adept at using them.

Consider what can be accomplished in just a few minutes of browsing Wikipedia, or searching Google's scanned repository of the world's out-of-copyright books. This is research of a range and rapidity beyond the wildest dreams of scholars just half a century ago, yet it now exists within the instant reach of almost any modern citizen. We are already as distant from that past as readers then were from the pre-Gutenberg world, where owning and reading books was restricted to an elite.

Unplugged from media's 'live' wires, however, our originality and rigour can come into play in a different and far older sense: our capacities to delegate, to make decisions, to act on our own initiative; to think without fear of pre-emption or a constant sense of an audience breathing down our necks. We are alone with ourselves, or present with each other, in a quite different sense than during any wired moment.

This is equally true in the personal and professional realms. In February 2011, I spoke at the London School of Economics alongside the author Lionel Shriver about the impact of new technologies on writing and thinking. She described the experience of writing 'with the crowd in your study' – that is, writing with the online reactions of your audience instantly and copiously visible – and the pressure this can create either to censor yourself or to try to please. 'I find that I need,' she said, 'to protect myself from other people's opinions', and described writing a newspaper column with her husband reading over her shoulder. 'You can't write that,' he said at one point, 'just look how they reacted to *that* last time online.'

This desire to protect ourselves is almost impossible to disentangle from the idea of knowing what that 'self' worth protecting is in the first place. Much of the rest of this book is devoted to the marvellous advances in collective thought and action that the technologies of the current century are already beginning to foster. Yet, more than ever, it is clear that we all also need some time in our lives for thinking our own thoughts without distraction, interruption or immediate feedback, even from those people we care about the most. It is also clear that, if we are not careful in guarding and managing such time, technology may take it from us.

In an age of constant live connections, the central question of self-examination is drifting from 'Who are you?' towards 'What are you doing?' Much as we may hunger for connection, if we are to thrive, we need to keep some sense of ourselves separate from this constant capacity to broadcast. We need tenses other than the present – other qualities of time – in our lives.

It's a point that was elegantly made by the computer scientist Jaron Lanier in a lecture at the South by Southwest conference in March 2010, during which he asked his audience to do nothing while he spoke other than listen. 'The most important reason to stop multi-tasking so much isn't to make me feel respected,' Lanier argued, 'but to make you exist. If you listen first, and write later, then whatever you write will have had time to filter through your brain, and you'll be in what you say. This is what makes you exist . . .'

As Lanier's plea for half an hour of 'unplugged' attention suggests, building unwired time into our lives is not a question of moving to a cabin on a mountainside or announcing a lifetime's exile from email – although it is telling that vacationing 'off grid' has become a fashionable form of indulgence for those who can afford it. Rather, unplugged time has the most to offer us as part of our every-day living: the decision not to send emails for a morning, to turn off all phones during a meeting or meal, to set some days or hours aside for off-grid reflection, or simply to meet someone in person rather than exchanging a twenty-email chain.

Like many of my contemporaries, I find myself increasingly trying to build units of unplugged productivity into my days: time with all my digital devices switched off, or carefully removed from my pocket. I find, too, that ease of continual contact and access has made personal meetings that much more significant. In the early 2000s, a technology conference often seemed to involve the most forward-thinking attendees ostentatiously using mobile phones and laptops throughout. Today, while no tech event is complete without a Twitter back-channel, it's also becoming common for speakers and chairs to request a version of Lanier's 'listen first, write later' principle. Conservatism, of a kind, is the new cutting edge.

On their own, such suggestions and trends do not constitute a manifesto. But they are the beginnings of an attitude that puts digital technology in its place: that defines a role for it within our lives, rather than making its presence merely a given fact of every moment.

Thanks to the staggering informational power of new media, time is more than ever our most precious resource. It is the one quantity of which all the world's technology cannot conjure a particle more – and whose experience it can threaten to turn into what the political theorist Fredric Jameson termed a 'perpetual present', in which society itself loses 'its capacity to retain its own past'.

For some people, the suffusion of the present is increasingly attended by strain and anxiety, and a sense of lost control. I have faith that we have not lost our capacity both to push back against and adapt within these transformations in our experience of time, either as a society or as individuals; and the next chapter explores these capacities for insight and change in more detail. Above all, though, every effort on our part should begin with the knowledge that without the ability to say 'no' as well as 'yes' to technology we risk turning its miracles into snares.

Time is the one quantity of which all the world's
technology cannot conjure a particle more.

3. Taking Control

I.

Few people could have predicted even a decade ago just how central the text message would become to a culture of smartphones, ubiquitous internet usage and tablets. According to research by Nielsen, based on the bills from over 60,000 mobile phone users in the US and over 3,000 separate customer surveys, American teenagers in 2010 were sending and receiving an average of 3,339 text messages every month – a figure peaking among females aged from 13 to 17, who averaged over 4,000. That works out at around 133 texts every day: more than seven messages for every single waking hour of the year.

The last chapter looked at the astonishing extent to which digital media fills many lives. With this comes not just complexity, but a parallel pressure to simplify – to regulate the endless streams of communication flowing our way. In this sense, texting is one of the most perfect tools yet developed for an age of information suffusion, for there is almost no simpler form of digital interaction than its bare numbers and letters. Composed, edited and re-composed at the sender's own pace, a text's final appearance gives away nothing of its making: no hesitations, slips, unintended implications or distractions. It's at once instant and asynchronous, requiring but not demanding attention. It asks almost as little as possible from all involved.

Texting's importance embodies an easily overlooked truth: that technology's theoretical possibilities are ultimately less important than convenience and control. If there's a warning here, it's that our growing need for convenience risks sacrificing control in a rather different sense: our capacity to ask more than a simplified minimum of both ourselves and others.

In George Clooney's 2011 political drama *The Ides of March*, the bedroom antics of members of a presidential-campaign team are repeatedly interrupted by breaking news, BlackBerry beeps and emails. It's a barbed gag for our times – and one that, increasingly, is not restricted to high-powered political workers. Those thousands of incoming text messages, like all digital updates, have little sympathy for any divisions of time and space we might wish to impose upon our days. Like Clooney's political animals, we may find that we are ranking the 'needs' of our machines above our own.

I have described the importance of thinking about wired and unwired time as two different resources in our lives. It's an easy thing to say, and a far harder thing to do. Yet establishing different kinds of time for different ways of being is vital on many levels: not just in terms of unplugging from media, but in differentiating between two quite distinct propositions – the best way to use a technological system, and the best way to live life itself.

Take one of the most telling words of our time, 'multitasking'. Within this term is encoded a set of assumptions that underpins many modern lives – the assumption that one of technology's greatest boons is the ability to perform several kinds of task simultaneously, and that thanks to this we are at our best and most efficient when we are weaving several streams of activity together.

Multitasking doesn't come easily to our minds. Can you focus on the vase and the faces at the same time?

In March 2007, this supposition was the subject of an article in the *New York Times*. Headlined 'Slow Down, Brave Multitasker, and Don't Read This in Traffic', a title that suggests the gist of its argument, the piece offered an unambiguous conclusion in the form of advice from David E. Meyer, a cognitive scientist and director of the Brain, Cognition and Action Laboratory at the University of Michigan. When it comes to almost any non-trivial operation, 'multitasking is going to slow you down, increasing the chances of mistakes . . . . Disruptions and interruptions are a bad deal from the standpoint of our ability to process information.'

In fact, the article suggested, the very idea of multitasking is something of a myth – a conclusion supported by considerable research both before and since from psychologists, neuroscientists and sociologists. Unlike machines, we humans do not have the capacity to thread our attention effortlessly between multiple complex tasks. Instead, we switch rapidly between them, not so much performing operations simultaneously as steadily dividing our attention into discrete packets.

When it comes to text messages and emails, this works very well much of the time. When it comes to the combination of these 'packets' of attention with anything requiring sustained mental effort, however, our all-round performance rapidly decays. According to internal research from Microsoft, for example, it took workers an average of a quarter of an hour to return to 'serious mental tasks' after replying to email or text messages. Once interrupted, they tended to stray off to deal with other messages or browse the web.

As early as 1998, the American writer Linda Stone coined the phrase 'continuous partial attention' to describe the idea of tracking information from several sources at the same time on a superficial level. This idea of shallow, shifting attention is probably a more accurate description for what many of us are doing much of the time than multitasking: performing a single sweeping mental operation across a range of sources, none of which we are able to give the individual attention a full 'task' demands.

Monitoring multiple sources of information is extremely powerful in some circumstances: when searching for data, following an unfolding event, co-ordinating a group of people, or simply ranging freely for inspiration or entertainment. It's a necessary skill for information-saturated lives. It isn't, however, the same thing as giving a complex idea your complete attention – or allowing yourself to engage deeply with the place you are in and the people you are sharing it with.

When, for example, I am sitting in a train checking my email, texting, Tweeting and listening to music, I am at once present and yet not all there. The world and the people around me are secondary to the events taking place on my screen. My attention is not only elsewhere, but distributed in fragments between shifting other places.

A new public propriety has evolved around this kind of partial attention. Plugged into your headphones, texting or talking or even filming what's around you, you occupy a stock role in the drama of digital living: the self-sufficient citizen, shielded from the dull restrictions of actuality by sound, visuals and friends on tap.

We respect this because it is part of the logic of modern living: an isolation that is the necessary counterpart to our ceaseless availability. It is essential to play this role from time to time. Yet the way in which it can slip from a temporary undertaking to a permanent way of being begs several important questions. What kind of attention do we deserve from those around us, or owe to them in return? And what kind of attention do we ourselves deserve, or need, if we are to be 'us' in the fullest possible sense?

2.

These questions concern not only those actions we attempt to perform simultaneously, but also how much we are prepared to delegate to digital technologies in our lives – and the degree to which we are willing to outsource not only communication, but an increasing number of aspects of ourselves.

Take memory. In a digital machine, 'memory' describes a binary sequence that encodes information. Limited but increasingly vast in capacity, the average memory of a computer today extends to many billions of digital bits: enough to encompass libraries of books, millions of images, weeks of film.

This kind of digital data storage is in some ways superior to a human memory. Computers' memories offer a complete, faithful and objective record of whatever is put into them. They do not degrade over time or introduce errors. They can be shared and copied almost endlessly without loss, or precisely erased if preferred. They can be fully indexed and rapidly searched. They can be remotely accessed and beamed across the world in fractions of a second, and their contents remixed, augmented or updated endlessly.

In computer terms, human memory is a poor thing: and it is in computing terms that we increasingly judge many aspects of

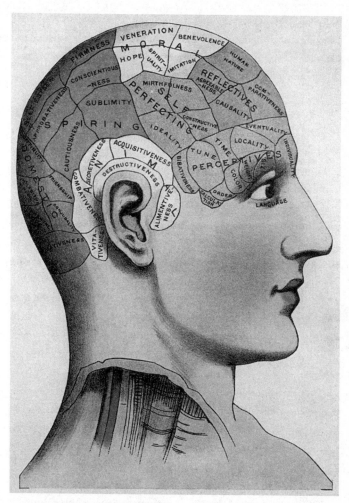

Despite the best hopes of Victorian science, human minds can't be boxed into compartments like a machine.

our mind. Predictably enough, we find them wanting, or no longer needed. From phone numbers and photographs to documents and diaries, we keep an increasingly vast quantity of memories important to our lives within machines: raw information, but also moments of feeling, of intimate exchange with friends and family.

I'm at an age when many of my friends are having their first children. It is, I've realized, a story my phone tells more clearly than any other object. Scrolling back through the last few years of those text messages I've kept, I can find six announcements of births, often sent within hours or even minutes of the event. They're similar enough to suggest a template: full name of the new arrival, time, weight in pounds and ounces, and an attached photograph.

It's a lovely thing to have. But scrolling through these messages also prompts an uneasy feeling in my chest, because I know why I've kept them there: without referring to them, I have no idea of the names or the birthdays of most of my close friends' firstborn children. I've replied to these texts, sometimes sent a card or gift as well, and then put the entire event out of mind. Despite the supplementary blogs, Facebook photos and network updates, these new arrivals seem barely to have impinged on my consciousness.

I am able to 'remember' these children's names in the same sense that I 'know' the phone numbers on my phone: the information is in my possession. It makes perfect sense for me to keep records like this, on a device that is almost always switched on in my pocket. Yet simply to speak of this as 'memory' risks a fundamental misunderstanding of what memories can signify to me as a human being – and of those aspects of the self, and of remembering, that cannot be outsourced to even the most sophisticated of devices.

Even the most comprehensive database lacks, for example, something that every human on earth takes for granted: a story. We are the products of our nature, but also of the unique experiences that reshape us throughout our lives. While we may identify the parts of our brain responsible for long- and short-term memories, there is no machine-simple memory module within us.

Indeed, there is no such thing as a human memory that exists outside of thought, feeling and selfhood. What we experience, do and learn becomes a part of us. We internalize events, people and ideas; we reflect, change our minds and misremember, possessing our pasts as a continuing part of our present. We cannot outsource our true memories any more than we can outsource our feelings or beliefs – nor can we separate them from 'us'.

As the author Nicholas Carr puts it in his 2010 book *The Shallows*, 'what gives real memory its richness and its character, not to mention its mystery and fragility, is its contingency. It exists in time, changing as the body changes . . . when we start using the Web as a substitute for personal memory, bypassing the inner processes of consolidation, we risk emptying our minds of their riches.'

Each computer and device may be unique, and have a unique history, but it is not this uniqueness that makes them what they are. Often, they function *despite* their histories, as anyone familiar with the symptoms of operating-system slowdown will know. For a machine, the past is a clogging burden. Classifying information neatly and keeping the operational sector clean is best. It's a fine lesson for the realm of work and productivity – but the exact inverse of what it takes to develop a well-stocked human mind.

3.

When we look at the nature and the quality of our interactions with those around us, the very systems that gift us control – email, text messages, status updates, social media – have the potential to denude us of what it means to thrive as human beings: shared history, depth of feeling, the acceptance of each others' uniqueness.

Yet despite the gloomy prognostications of critics like Carr, this does not have to be the case. For what are at stake here are not simply different modes of attention and memory, but the different ways of thinking that lie beneath these: a field within which we humans retain a remarkable ability to adapt, and to take proper ownership of what's going on inside our heads.

Consider the emerging field known in computer science as 'memory engineering'. Designed to address the immense overload of digital information we all leave behind us, its approach is not brute aggregation, but rather the desire to humanize this data – and to convert it from inert electronic stuff to something more esoteric, differentiated and deeply felt.

A New York-based programmer, Jonathan Wegener, has, for example, helped invent a service that highlights things within our digital trails that happened exactly a year ago: called PastPosts, it uses Facebook to 'bring back' activity that happened exactly a year ago on our accounts. Operating under the slogan 'What did you do a year ago today on Facebook?', it's a simple idea, but one that highlights how easy it can be to assert the shape of an individual human history within an undifferentiated electronic record.

Data, after all, is only inert if we allow it to remain so. I look at my friends' Facebook pages, their websites, even their video-game avatars, and I see not something anti-human, but the repeated assertion of individual control. Ending a relationship via text message may well be cruel and cowardly; but a son's birth announced on a social-networking site, trailed by a hundred well-wishing comments from friends and family, diminishes no one. Similarly, the internet now positively bristles with applications and advice for aiding focus on a single task, with techniques ranging from a program able to cut off all a computer's network connections for a fixed time to 'dark room' word processors that reduce the display to a black background and the words being typed.

Perhaps the most challenging mental state of all to cultivate in a digital age, however, is very different to both the quick-fire reflexivity of partial attention and the absolute focus of pure attention: those freeform reveries associated with both creative insight and personal peacefulness.

The kind of thoughts that can emerge in 'empty' time in our lives – on a train, in the bath, walking, glancing out of a window between turning the pages of a book – are impossible to reproduce either through dedicated digital planning or carefully arranged offline sessions. They are moments that steal up on us, most often, when life is not segmented down to the minute. They are idiosyncratic, individual and serendipitous – a kind of freedom granted, in the words of the British Enlightenment philosopher John Locke's *Essay Concerning Human Understanding*, 'when ideas float in our mind, without any reflection or regard of the understanding'.

In the context of this chapter – of taking control and understanding the nature of our attention – this suggests an important note of caution: that all systems and strategies need some space for eccentricity. For our thoughts to be entirely our own, we need freedom not simply from the tyranny of misused tools, but also from even our own best demands and strategies.

During the writing of this book, I found myself feeling the force of this. When I write steadily onto paper with a pen, as I chose to do for much of my drafting, words flow with the sense that they exist just half a sentence ahead of the nib. The mechanical slowness of writing helps me feel them as sounds and objects as well as ideas, creating a synaesthetic and sensuous pleasure in their arrival. Carefully composing like this into a physical notebook helps my processes of writing and reverie to mix, often unexpectedly: sentences and phrases suddenly arriving after moments of wandering thought.

This is perhaps why I also rely for inspiration on writing notes in the margins of physical books: texts I carry around and like to read uninterrupted, waiting for inspiration to creep out of the reading process. Flicking back through these books, the moments at which my ideas snapped into focus are marked by strings of bad handwriting diving across the pages.

These acts – reading with a pen in my hand, walking with a notebook in my bag – grant me licence to let my mind wander. I have come to think of them as a luxurious yet necessary process for turning my work into something that both has rigour and belongs to me alone.

My onscreen writing, by contrast, is more about re-reading and the architecture of paragraphs and arguments: both necessary disciplines, but far more vulnerable to the temptations of partial attention

The author's own notebooks and marginalia: a semi-legible licence to let attention wander.

and online browsing. At my computer, typing, I find it easy to let present distractions push an anxious backlog of other ideas to the edges of my attention. For as long as I'm editing, typing, researching and checking the odd email, I can remain in denial. Then I step away from the screen, and what I really ought to be concerned about begins to rise up.

My own working methods are not a template or an ideal. They don't always work for me, let alone others. But they do, I hope, provide a practical example of what it can mean to prevent the logic of digital tools from wholly dictating the logic of thought: the way that different types and textures of time can help us to draw ourselves out, rather than narrow down to a single attitude.

We must be able to adapt to circumstances – and to adapt our circumstances to us, insisting that they accommodate the full gamut of our observing, thinking and feeling. This includes the capacity to divide our attention; or to devote ourselves to one idea, or to one another, to the exclusion of all others. But there must also be time and space for other freedoms – and for us to work in ways whose only necessary justification is that they work for us.

4. Reframing Technology

I.

In the summer of 2010, I made my first visit to the headquarters of a company that for years had been a constant part of my life: Google. Even though I'd visited its offices in London before, I had never really thought of Google as something that takes up physical space in the way that a bank or a shop does. The Googleplex – 1600 Amphitheatre Parkway, Mountain View, California – changed all that. Today, looking at the Google search bar lodged in the top-right corner of my internet browser, I imagine a place, faces and a history overlaying its text.

Google's home is a campus, and being there is a 'total' experience: if you work there, you can enjoy a gymnasium, sunny courtyards, beach volleyball, tech toys, laundry facilities and three meals a day on site. As one employee explained it, workers are treated 'like adults' – trusted to work and play hard, pursuing their projects in their own time. In another sense, this also means they are treated like school-children, or at least like members of a politely paternal institution – liberated from mundane concerns the better to learn and perform.

In the endless bright space of the outer San Francisco Bay, between distant mountains and gridded freeways, it made a Platonic kind of sense. There was, I felt by the end of my time in California, more than a hint of the Renaissance city state to both Google and its great Californian colleague, Apple. Each is a place of extraordinary

Silicon Valley at sunset: even world-spaning digital services are born from a particular place and time.

cultural fertility, complete with its own aesthetic and attitude: the relentlessly minimal modernism of Apple, where users' needs and whims are pre-empted with a commitment to elegance that borders on the pathological; the Technicolor postmodernism of Google, whose software tools are ceaselessly calibrated to make anything that anyone might ever wish to know discoverable.

There's also a brute business logic to all of this – focused, at Google, on the relentless cataloguing and interrogation of data, and the massively profitable matching of advertising to particular search terms. I knew much of this, in the abstract, before I spent any time at the company's physical headquarters. Having both visited and spent some time experiencing its culture, however, I began to realize just how much I had been missing.

For me, as for so many other people, Google had been first and foremost a tool and a verb. It's a company whose ethos focuses on ease, efficiency and seamlessness, and I had used it as intended: gratefully, effortlessly and largely unquestioningly. Yet here was a place with a history, a faith. Behind the beautiful algorithmic mechanics of its product were brilliant, biased, imperfect people, just as there are behind every program, every product and every anonymous interface. There were debates and mixed feelings about what the company ought to be doing next; known issues and little-known triumphs; a bewildered frustration at the 'Google is making us stupid' lobby of journalistic thinking.

All manufactured objects alienate us from the circumstances of their production. Handling something as complex and compact as a mobile phone, it's hard to hold in mind the snaking chains of supply and manufacture that have brought it into being: the mining of metals for circuits and batteries; the distillation of oil into high-performance plastics; the factory labour and software engineering; the design and prototyping and patents.

With an onscreen object like Google's search engine, the alienation is still more complete. Within the anonymous pixels of identical screens across the world, I encounter their service as if it were something found rather than made. It is everywhere and nowhere: part of an organic 'landscape' or 'ecosystem', to use two of the most commonly deployed terms in the new-media vocabulary. Services like Google or Amazon don't look as if they were created by people in the same sense as the phone in my pocket, let alone the shoes on my feet. And so my capacity to critique, to interpret and to 'see' them in the same sense as I see the world of objects around me diminishes – and my use of them slides towards habit rather than critical engagement.

This isn't a criticism of Google. Rather, it's a criticism of the tendency to treat digital services and devices as though they are natural or inevitable: things existing outside of history and human error in a media 'landscape' that we must simply navigate as best we can. For Google and Amazon are every bit as manmade as a pair of jeans or a Duracell battery. And behind their seemingly ineffable existences are historical and human contexts, ripe for debate.

2.

In March 2010, I reported for the *Observer* newspaper on the efforts of the British broadcaster Channel 4's education arm to create an online game that would help young people to explore what it means to use social networks like Facebook safely and effectively. As part of its research, the developers commissioned by Channel 4 to make the game – a London-based firm called Six to Start – spoke to groups of pupils at schools in the south of England.

What soon became clear during the course of these conversations was that, while technology played a central role in almost every teen's socializing, work and leisure, their expertise fell far short of most adult assumptions. In Donald Rumsfeld's immortal words, a host of 'unknown unknowns' lurked behind almost every media experience – a list of things they didn't even know they didn't know.

Top of most pupil's lists were privacy settings. 'Almost every teen we've talked to feels that they know everything about issues like online privacy, identity and security,' Adrian Hon, chief creative officer at Six to Start, told me, 'and the fact that most adults they've heard from insist on scaremongering about paedophiles means they're no longer interested in what adults have to say.' Teens' real fears and vulnerabilities lay not in upfront sexual approaches by strangers but in the mire of privacy settings, tagged photographs, mobile-phone numbers and dates of birth.

Most children, Hon found, 'are worried about bullying online, and in a more general sense, their position in the social order. I also noticed that many had a vague, hard-to-articulate sense of unease about what people might know about them online. Facebook's privacy settings seem to change every few months and it was hard for even us to figure out what they all meant . . .'

This is the human flip-side to the assumption that a younger generation are gladly and seamlessly transposing much of their lives into the digital. As some parents are becoming increasingly aware, the role of technology in teens' lives comes with its own anxieties, uncertainties and nagging questions – and the fact that these are seldom officially broached does little to help anyone involved.

The game Hon's team developed, Smokescreen, won the award for Best Game at the 2010 South by Southwest festival, thanks largely to its honesty in acknowledging these problems. Successive missions cast players in the role of teenagers watching events like a party with open online invitations spiralling out of control, or someone fighting to stop embarrassing photographs of themselves damaging their school career. It's simple enough stuff. Yet most adult social-network users would fall down on many of the tasks in question.

As Hon sees it, teens are willing to learn more about the dangers of the digital world, and even passionately interested in doing so: the problem is that the way these discussions are usually delivered to them is 'just not credible'. Sex claims the headlines – and becomes a running joke in classrooms – while less sensational concerns go unaddressed. What is needed, Hon argues, is something credible and engaging that can get across a general lesson for online behaviour: along the lines of 'be smart, and take a moment to think about the consequences of what you're doing'.

I would make a still larger claim: that there's a strong case to be made for the study and debate of digital media to be a compulsory part of the world's education systems, alongside literacy, numeracy and science. This doesn't mean the kind of all-too-basic 'how to' guides that leave media-savvy students cold, but rather a combination of digital history with opportunities to debate the realities and limitations of everything from social-media services and search engines to avatars and World of Warcraft. Above all, this should mean generations meeting on common ground – and listening to, as well as telling, stories about the digital world as they are each experiencing it.

3.

This chapter began with an account of a visit to Google: a company founded in California in 1998. When it comes to many of the most basic components of the digital world, however – from the idea of an electronic filing system to the protocols that govern the World Wide Web – there is often no physical entity to visualize, and no easy human story to unearth.

Even with the resources of the internet at your disposal, for example, it's difficult to find out exactly why almost every modern digital device stores information in a system of distinct 'files'. And unless you're a computer scientist, it's almost impossible to debate the benefits and drawbacks of this system, or to consider what other kinds of system might have been used instead, or might be used in the future.

This is true to a degree of all complex technologies. When it comes to digital technologies, however, both the influence and the invisibility of these 'locked-in' ideas is especially significant. As the author Jaron Lanier highlights in his book *You Are Not A Gadget*, even something as seemingly simple as the storage of records is contingent on particular technological formats and devices. A book, movie or song stored as a computer file is not like a physical record: without the appropriate software and hardware to convert its data back into sounds and pictures, it is inert.

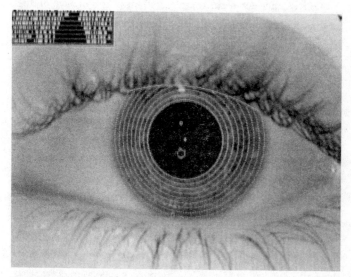

Blink and you'll miss them: understanding technologies' problems and potentials is getting tougher all the time.

Accessing such technologies has never been easier. Yet understanding them is getting harder all the time; a process that many manufacturers are both aware of and willing tacitly to encourage, selling devices and services that work straight out of the box, with little opportunity for users either to customize their own experience or to see beneath the surface into what is going on inside.

Convenience and security are part of the charm of such devices, and the loss of certain kinds of control may well be a price worth paying – so long as buyers are aware that a price *is* being paid. From hardware to software, however, this kind of awareness is often in short supply. Endless unread pages of End User Licence Agreements specify what rights are being signed away when we use many services; purchase agreements specify that many digital products are not actually owned by their buyers, merely licensed. In each case, if the appropriate service or support is revoked, inert and unusable information is all that remains.

Grasping these contexts is a serious challenge, not least because it can seriously obstruct the casual daily business of simply using digital products and services. It's worth remembering, though, that unless some scrutiny is brought to bear on the intentions and limitations encoded within our tools, we can only expect fewer improvements and more abuses to occur. As John Naughton, professor of the public understanding of technology at the Open University, put it in a November 2011 article for the *Observer*, 'if you use "free" services then what you have to accept is that you (or, more precisely, your identity) are their product.' There is no such thing as something for nothing, even online.

We may live in an age of services and devices that seem closer to an ecology than to mere machinery – and it may suit their makers for us to treat them as such – but the only nature that has moulded these technologies is our own. And if we ourselves are not able to grasp the histories and complexities behind the digital world's ever-shifting scenery, we can nevertheless reach out to those who have done – and to their critiques, warnings, endorsements and alternatives.

You may be unlikely to come up with an alternative to Facebook overnight, or an Amazon-beating online retailer. But you might learn to use each a little better – and to consider what it is that even these giants can't do for you.

5. Sharing, Expertise and the End of Authority

I.

In 1998, two students at Stanford University published a paper titled 'The Anatomy of a Large-Scale Hypertextual Web Search Engine'. Behind this dry summary lay what would prove one of the digital era's most significant ideas: how to bring a new principle of discernment to bear on the world's increasingly massive, diverse online repositories of information.

How, the authors asked, was it possible to combine an 'uncontrolled' medium 'where anyone can publish anything they want' with truly satisfying search results, telling users not just where to find information, but also which information was most likely to be accurate and useful? Their answer – and their belief that such an answer not only existed, but could be scaled up to address billions of published documents – would help profoundly to change the world over the ensuing decade.

The study's authors were Sergei Brin and Larry Page, and their proposal was for a product they christened Google – a playful variation on the mathematical term 'googol', a one followed by a hundred zeros. Web search engines had existed since the start of the 1990s. Brin and Page, however, noted that little research had been done in attempting to improve the quality of the results they offered. Their most significant innovation came from the insight that the methodology of academic research itself suggested a solution to this.

In academia, it has long been true that the number of citations a piece of work receives provides a proxy for its authority within a field. A piece of research that is referenced in a hundred subsequent papers can self-evidently be considered more authoritative than one that is never referred to by anyone. Similarly, Brin and Page reasoned, the number of times that a page on the World Wide Web was linked to by other pages offered a useful insight into its importance or quality – and was, moreover, an assessment that could automatically be conducted by a sufficiently sophisticated algorithm.

The algorithm outlined in the paper was christened 'PageRank' – and it still exists today at the core of what has become perhaps the world's single most influential digital service. PageRank has grown immensely in sophistication since those early days, and its exact formulation is a closely guarded corporate secret. Its guiding principle, however, remains the same. Sufficiently precise mass observation can provide the key to that most elusive of qualities – quality itself.

Rather than requiring its creators to assess the quality of online resources, an algorithm like PageRank automatically observes how everybody else is using and constructing the web. Key variables include a website's number of incoming links, the number of visitors it receives, the frequency with which it is updated, and the kind of content within it. On top of this are layered sophisticated indices including the kind of visitors a site receives, how long and deeply they engage with it, the relative authority of all the different sites connected to it, and whether any kind of suspicious behaviour is taking place that suggests someone may be trying artificially to boost its ranking.

Only the most distinguished French citizens can be interred in the Panthéon in Paris. In a digital world, what does the best mean?

The stories of Google's and other search engines' increasingly advanced statistical analyses, and their arms race with those attempting to bias results, are fascinating tales in their own right. Still more significant, however, is the cultural shift of which these are emblematic. For in the space of just over a decade, innovations in processing ever huger data sets have shifted our sense of what authority means further than during any comparable period in history – at the same time challenging some of our most central notions of cultural and intellectual value.

2.

The word 'authority' first entered the English language in the early thirteenth century, arriving from Old French with specifically bookish connotations. An 'auctorite', as it was commonly spelt, was a text in which one could have faith – and which you could thus use as the basis of cultural and theological arguments. The ultimate text of this kind was the Bible, followed by the most venerated of classical and religious authors. Such texts were their own guarantees of accuracy, and the highest form of scholarship and critical thought involved teasing out their meanings and applying these to the world.

Deference to authority was not simply a matter of custom; it was the basis of an entire political and intellectual system. Over time, an 'authority' came also to mean someone steeped in book learning who could be considered an expert, or someone who through their position – a lord, a monarch, an abbot – merited others' obedience. In each case, a kind of faith was embodied in the act of deference: faith, as much as anything, in the idea that such deference was a social and cultural good.

The Enlightenment, democratization and mass culture have long since diluted such tendencies. Yet a certain degree of faith in expertise has remained a constant part of cultural life, with the twinned figures of the critic and the creator at its core. Outside of the scientific method's empirical realm (which itself is being radically transformed by the power of massive data sets), we have long tolerated – even demanded – people whose role it is to advise us about what we should like and dislike, who attempt both to embody and to educate public taste, battling towards the canon of whatever is best within a field.

Even the most educated criticism has always been just one factor among many. We have long known which books sell most, which films have the biggest audiences, which works of art fetch the highest prices, who wins the most votes. What we never had until a decade or so ago, however, is the radically new scale and species of empiricism embodied in the internet. At our fingertips today lies instant access to a far more subtle and ubiquitous kind of popularity contest than any bestseller list: one attached in a constantly evolving form to almost every single form of enquiry it is possible to undertake.

There is almost no word or phrase in any language for which a modern search engine will not display, and rank, results. Thanks to services like Amazon, there is also almost no such thing as a product – whether cultural or commercial – that does not come with its number of sales helpfully ranked from one to many million, and the ratings and opinions of previous consumers appended only a click away. We still relish critical opinions and the clashes between them. But when everyone is able not only to have their opinion, but to broadcast it, merely individual claims of expertise can start looking flimsy to the point of translucency.

Consider what exactly it means to search for something online. It's easy enough to accept that information like the height of a mountain or the population of a country has an empirical value. Increasingly, though, questions like 'Was Picasso the greatest artist of the twentieth century?' have also taken on an empirical tinge. Simply ask the internet, and the world's answers will be laid out before you, ranked in order of relevance. The aggregated information is at your fingertips: not in the form of a single answer, but rather in a definitive response to the implicit question 'What are all the things that people have said about Picasso being the twentieth century's greatest artist – and which of these things are most authoritative?'

The formulation may be cumbersome, but this is precisely the kind of judgement that we have traditionally turned to critics for; and not only to critics, but to gatekeepers of all kinds, from publishers to editors and educators. For centuries, it has been the case that no one can individually possess, consume or meaningfully search even a fraction of the world's knowledge. So we have always turned to others to advise and to select materials for us – and to determine what gains entry to those fields of permanent record in the first place.

Today, the process of selection is no longer one that happens before something is sent into the world. Rather, it is an ongoing, outsourced business. Almost anything and everything is now in front of the world's gaze, sifted not by gatekeepers but by public taste. Indeed, this is the beating heart of most digital business models. Instead of first selecting and then publishing, you publish first and then respond to the world's own selections – relentlessly maximizing those things that win an audience, and wasting little effort on those that don't.

3.

If this is a crisis of values and authority, it is in many ways an extraordinarily benign one: the opening-up of once daunting citadels. There are, however, two particular areas of concern for those aiming to do more than simply drift within culture's new direction: the intellectual and the economic.

Intellectually, the concern is one of flattening: the collapse of notions of excellence into a mulch of amateurism and self-promotion. Authors like the American writer Andrew Keen have argued that – as the subtitle of his 2007 book *The Cult of the Amateur* puts it – 'today's internet is killing our culture', the culture in question being something propagated and safeguarded by discerning gatekeepers, working in concert with intellectuals and artists.

From book and magazine publishing to music, cinema and political discourse, Keen argues, digital technology's suffusion is debasing the capacity of the exceptional and the meaningful to have public impact or provide a focus for debate. Instead, we skip at whim across the trivial and the profound alike – lingering for longest on the most digestible morsels.

Keen's argument is a version of ancient concerns over democratization writ large. In replacing expert filtering with mass access, Keen argues, the internet has gifted power to human nature in its mob form: drowning out dissenting or exceptional voices, sweeping along a passive majority with easily digestible arguments and pandering to popular culture.

Coupled to this cultural critique comes an economic argument that will be grimly familiar to anyone involved in a traditional media business over the last decade – perhaps most recently and forcefully articulated in the American author Robert Levine's 2011 book *Free Ride*. Revealingly subtitled – 'How Digital Parasites are Destroying the Culture Business, and How the Culture Business Can Fight Back' – *Free Ride* delves into the structure of the modern 'culture industries' and the damage that has been done to their business models by digital technologies. 'Traditional media companies aren't in trouble because they're not giving consumers what they want,' Levine observes, 'they're in trouble because they can't collect money for it.' The digital embrace of concepts like 'open' and 'free' may be hard to argue with in principle, he points out, but what they can mean in practice is the privileging of infrastructure at the expense of allowing creators any control over what they make – let alone making a living.

It's possible to split hairs and dispute the statistical details of old media's collapse. Yet few people would seriously dispute that massive damage has been done both to many existing business models and to cultural assumptions by the emergence of digital media. The real question at stake is not so much what is taking place as how much it matters.

It's at this point that Levine's thesis dovetails most compellingly with Keen's. From their perspective, digital technology has transferred both economic and social influence away from those engaged in creating cultural and intellectual works, and towards those controlling the infrastructure through which all media and ideas increasingly flow. Much as online authority has increasingly become divorced from expertise, so, it seems, cultural production is becoming divorced from talent.

This sounds like a deeply disturbing proposition for anyone who cares about quality as well as quantity – and it is one that points towards one of the most uncomfortable paradoxes of a digital world: those ways in which diversity and openness have enhanced rather than undermined the influence of a small number of players.

Where once the number of objects competing for an audience's attention numbered in the thousands, it now runs beyond the millions. The digital environment is rich with new opportunities for anyone occupying a sufficiently well-defined niche: the 'long tail' of minority interests. Yet perhaps the most noticeable impact of the shift in scale has been not diversity, but the growth of an ever more influential minority at the top. Much as companies like Amazon and eBay are able, online, to attain a global dominance almost inconceivable in the pre-digital era, so battles of culture and ideas are more than ever dominated by those few that succeed in winning mass attention.

There's something brutally Darwinian about this kind of competition. Take books. If you are holding the physical, non-digital version of this book, you are holding a single-purpose object: one designed exclusively to present these words to its readers. If, however, you are reading these words on the screen of a device like an iPad, then they will be occupying the same physical space not only as every other digital text in your library, but as every other piece of music, film, news, blogging and video gaming you use.

It's in the nature of a digital era that these things come at us increasingly in parallel, through the same channels, consumed simultaneously or in seamless sequence. Only the strong, it seems, will survive. And this is a strength measured not by a critical gaze with one eye fixed on eternity – even in the case of those works that have endured in a field for long enough to be considered classics. Rather, it's a strength drawn from the new authority of the measured majority.

4.

If this was all there was to our online behaviour, the present would be grim indeed for those hoping to do more than drift. Yet I believe that arguments like Keen's and Levine's are best read as warnings rather than inexorable fates – and that, while many traditional business models may be doomed, our established notions of excellence, critical insight and creative spark will not so easily fall by the wayside.

Algorithms are able to aggregate human behaviour on an inhuman scale. This is the source of their utility and power. Yet this loss of individual human scale is also their greatest omission – and one of the central reasons that since the founding of Facebook in 2004 and Twitter in 2006, these two services alone have between them amassed over a billion users. Once again, the numbers involved are huge. Yet this latest wave of digital developments is as much predicated on intimacy and individual agency as on the power of the majority: of internet users not just as faceless consumers of mass culture, but as individuals actively engaged in mass cultural and intellectual production.

Writing in September 2010, the American writer and senior editor at the *Atlantic* magazine, Alexis Madrigal, described Twitter as 'a kind of human recommendation engine in which I am the algorithm'. It's one of the most suggestive explanations I've found yet as to why social media have so drastically and rapidly reshaped the dynamics of the internet. They answer to a particular need that algorithms alone cannot serve: the opportunity to speak, and listen to others, from that unique position of authority each one of us occupies – as an authority on our own place in the world.

Today, we are all broadcasters and commentators – just as we are also diarists, radio hosts, critics, comforters, voyeurs, and our own full-time publicists. The key question, then, is how well we are able to perform in these roles. What makes for a culture of sharing in which the values we associate with thriving can flourish rather than be stifled? And what space is there for those who wish to speak of qualitative as well as quantitative differences?

In answering these questions, we have the best hope of succeeding if we can reapply for the twenty-first century those principles that have always driven worthwhile critical discourse: respect not for authority in itself, but for the principles of honest argument, articulate self-awareness, and a genuine desire to learn.

Consider how the dynamics of this sharing played out around one sombre recent event: the execution by lethal injection of an American man convicted of murder in the state of Georgia. On 21 September 2011, forty-two-year-old Troy Davis was put to death for a crime committed twenty-two years previously: the murder of a police officer in Savannah, Georgia, in August 1989.

Throughout the two decades between the murder and the execution, Davis maintained his innocence, supported by an increasingly broad range of human-rights groups, public figures and political leaders. Debate around the case hinged on the absence of a murder weapon, the fact that seven out of nine prosecution witnesses subsequently recanted their evidence, allegations of police coercion, and the possibility that the key witness against Davis was himself the murderer.

Davis's execution was delayed three times, but all petitions and appeals were ultimately denied. The way the world experienced the end of Davis's story, though, could not have been more different to its beginnings. From a last-minute appeal to the Supreme Court and an appeal for clemency that gathered over 600,000 signatures, including those of both the Pope and a former head of the FBI, the last days and hours of Davis's life were not simply rolling news on television, but a rolling global outpouring of anger, argument and anguish.

From my study desk in London, I watched the words fly across Twitter far faster than it was possible to read them: many millions of words from hundreds of thousands of participants, ranging from Salman Rushdie ('America looks a little uglier tonight') and Alec Baldwin ('US death penalty humiliates us in the eyes of much of the world') to those never likely to publish a book or act in a film, but speaking out equally as themselves.

As the author Andrew O'Hagan put it, writing the next week in the *London Review of Books*, 'the vigil-keepers and the writers are one . . . this is how news happens now: there is no delay between the event and its reception, between the deed, the word, and the spreading of the word'. For all the cacophony, what I found on my screen was not incoherence or mob rule. Rather, it read like the world thinking to itself, filtered through the gazes of those whose outlooks I have come to trust and respect.

Alongside the stream of Twitter comments, I followed links and recommendations from the hundred or so people I have chosen personally to follow over the last two years: people ranging from friends and colleagues to authors, judges, artists, entrepreneurs, doctors and teachers. These sent me in turn to blogs and newspapers; to images and debates and comment threads; to forums and petitions and activist sites. The effect was multiple, yet not incoherent. Guided by those I trust, I watched the debate ripple and resound, passing on the best insights I found to those who follow me in turn.

There were no final words to be found here, and nothing like the tidy closure of a traditional news 'event'. Returning to the #TroyDavis hashtag on Twitter at the start of the next month, I found one update or more still appearing each minute, mapping not so much a live event as the thousands of ways in which that event continued to be *lived* – in which it had become a part of individual lives around the world. There were voices from his funeral; old arguments, comebacks and controversies; insults, abuse, and the continuing echoes of the most resonant comments from the days and months before.

Some have argued that this weight of mass articulacy is doomed to be dominated by rumours, half-truths and special-interest groups: that, in the words of the American author and academic Cass Sunstein, a future of mass sharing is most likely to be an 'echo chamber' of like-minded people reinforcing their own beliefs and prejudices.

This echoes Andrew Keen's criticisms of digital culture in general, and of its potential for pandering, apathy and drowning out truth and excellence: warnings eminently worth heeding. Yet to claim them as the whole truth seems to me to be both too pessimistic and too passive a perspective – and a misreading of the individual agency that remains within even the largest online collectives.

When it comes to authority, and to notions of excellence defined by critical insight rather than statistical analysis, we cannot turn the clock back to an era of pre-digital gatekeepers safeguarding – and moulding – public taste. We are, however, increasingly able to seek out and propagate this kind of discernment outside the monoliths of search engines and aggregation; to share not only trivia, but also evidence that values other than mob euphoria are meaningful to the many as well as the few.

When it comes to thriving, moreover, the digital realm has already amply proved itself a cornucopia for high as well as low. It may be a lean time for seasoned professionals and media production; for passionate amateurs and emerging talents alike, however, the opportunities have never been greater, even if the certainties are few.

One recent venture, for example, was launched in 2011 under the name Unbound Books, offering writers a platform for pitching their ideas directly to the reading public. Much like the eighteenth-century model of securing advance publishing subscriptions, if Unbound's authors manage to persuade a certain number of readers to pledge their financial support for the proposed book, they can then get writing and end up with a complete book – one professionally produced by Unbound and sent direct to their readers.

It's a minor example; yet it also represents an act of faith in the capacity of a digital public to be much more than any mob. In the words of Noam Chomsky, an early admirer of the Unbound Model, 'the significance could be quite substantial' – especially if such schemes are the shape of new businesses to come, and of business models where profits are not simply inimical to quality.

In all such acts of sharing and cultural investment, the cardinal virtues are trust and respect: the foundations of earned authority in a communal age. Over four hundred years ago, Shakespeare's Hotspur knew the value of reputation in an era when a good man's word was his bond. Across the ensuing centuries, entrepreneurial authors helped build high and low literary cultures alike through their assiduous courting of audiences.

Today, we are learning a version of that lesson again. The world is as full of experts as it ever was. But they and their audience are newly equal in the business of striving to articulate and promote excellence itself: newly reliant on each others' trust, and increasingly unable to rely upon any notion of authority as something bestowed by an institution or position rather than won on the field of debate.

Economically and socially, it is a fragile time to care about culture as it was once conceived. Yet we need more than ever to be able to discern – and to learn those habits that will allow us to do so together.

6. On Becoming Less than Human

I.

Pornography, wrote J.G. Ballard in the foreword to his 1973 novel *Crash*, is 'the most political form of fiction, dealing with how we use and exploit each other, in the most urgent and ruthless way'. It was an exploitation he linked explicitly to technology, appending to this most disturbing of his fictions a question that has only become more pointed over the four decades since: 'Do we see, in the car-crash, the portents of a nightmare marriage between technology, and our own sexuality? . . . Is there some deviant logic unfolding here, more powerful than that provided by reason?'

No account of living with technology would be complete without taking sexuality into account; and the most obvious place to begin exploring the 'deviant logic' of their melding is the astounding volume of pornography to be found on digital networks today.

Contrary to popular belief, 'sex' is not the most searched-for term on the internet. If you ask Google about 'sex', it will offer just under two and a half billion results: enough to beat most enquiries but, charmingly, still less than a third of the more than seven billion results for 'love'. The key point, though, is not how much raw material is available, but how accessible it is. Online, you are never more than a search and a click away from porn. What was once a taboo – requiring a visit to a specialist retailer, bounded by age and access restrictions

– is now mundane. If you want pornography, you can get it: instantly, anonymously, free of both monetary and emotional cost. And in this, pornography is almost exactly like everything else in the digital realm. It's normal, in the sense that it's just another part of the service.

Pornography has itself been altered by the internet. For a start, it has lost whatever residual innocence or coyness it may once have had. Like every other part of the entertainment industry, porn is now in competition with both itself and everything else. This means that an ineffably lowest-common-denominator business has generally become still cheaper, nastier and more ingenious in outdoing itself – and the distinction more blurred between consumption and participation, staged and real.

Not only are you never more than a click away from most things you can think of online; you are also never alone. No matter how bizarre, unusual, eclectic or even illegal your tastes – in matters of sex and pretty much anything else – there will be others like you out there, armed with advice, forums, systems for meeting, and discrete security protocols as needed. Tell the world what you want and, if the world also contains someone who'd like to give it to you, it's likely that technology can bring you together.

Consider the 'personals' section of the world's most successful classified advertising website, Craigslist. This section comes, today, in nine flavours: platonic, women seeking women, women seeking men, men seeking women, men seeking men, misc romance, casual encounters, 'missed connections' (for winning the attention of someone you've seen around) and 'rants and raves' (for praise and abuse).

As these pragmatic and comprehensive categories suggest, practically everything legal and conceivable is catered for. The site does

This probably wouldn't get you very far on AdultFriendFinder.com.

prominently offer personal-safety tips, advice on avoiding scams and frauds, and information on how to obtain parental-control software, and it has a strong anti-prostitution and -trafficking policy. Beyond this, though, you're free simply to get on with it. Click on the category appropriate to your tastes, and you'll be taken through to a chronological listing of people in your area advertising their needs, or what they're willing to provide.

In London, my home city, a typical day on the Craigslist personals might see around 900 new entries in the casual-encounters section, 200 in men seeking men, 100 in men seeking women, 50 in women seeking men, and between 2 and 25 in the rest. Almost all are frighteningly or refreshingly frank, depending on your perspective ('must have a very large disposable income to spoil me with or i won't reply', 'nice guy available on tuesday in the morning? get back to me with photo in first email and location otherwise no reply'). And almost all need little more than a mouse-click and email to follow up.

A more provincial location reduces these totals to only a handful of locals each week – perhaps necessitating, for the dedicated seeker or servicer, the charms of a more specialized site like AdultFriend-Finder, 'the world's largest sex & swinger personals community'. Such a tagline may stretch the credibility of the word 'community', but the purity of the common interest at stake couldn't be clearer. Like almost everything else in an age of ubiquitous technology, digital sex isn't just about looking: it's about seeking, connecting, and finding that you're not alone – or that aloneness need no longer be dull if you have an internet connection.

It's also about getting exactly what you want, when you want it. Fancy an affair with no strings attached, no chance of ruining your marriage, and discretion guaranteed? Simply seek out a like-minded adulterer on a site like Illicit Encounters, 'The UK's Largest Married Dating Site', complete with advice on how to avoid detection. Fancy the company of a hairy man three times your body weight? There are sites for that too (the key search-engine term being 'bear').

2.

There's plenty to celebrate in helping people get what they want – even if you suspect it isn't always what they need. The concerns that this breeds, though, run in two related directions.

First, there is the potential for people to suffer harm at the hands of others: a possibility that is both alarming and morally clear-cut. From the exploitation of the vulnerable to trading in illicit materials, the digital combination of distance, anonymity and concealment can be a toxic mix. Sexual abuse, trafficking and illegal forms of pornography are just one aspect of digital networks' dark side, but they are among its most disturbing and headline-grabbing manifestations, and must be both legislated and guarded against – something technology has both facilitated and made more challenging.

Horrifying though these abuses are, they are also relatively rare. Second, however, is a concern at once more widespread and morally ambiguous: that a large number of people may suffer damage to their quality of life thanks to the frictionless ease of exploitative, reductive and potentially addictive digital behaviours.

Sexuality, here, is an emblem of larger and more nebulous fears – about our capacity onscreen to turn each other into objects, to coarsen our own sensibilities, and to retreat from the risks and rewards of fuller human contact. In a 2010 piece in the journal *The New Atlantis*, the British philosopher Roger Scruton memorably characterized this process of 'hiding behind the screen' as 'a process of alienation whereby people learn to . . . make their lives into playthings over which they retain complete, though in some way deeply specious, control.' Scruton acknowledged that not all digital interactions entail such reduction, but offered a warning against the ways in which our freedom to live as fully human beings is damaged when we cut ourselves off from 'the world of human relations . . . with its risks, conflicts, and responsibilities'.

Ease and instant gratification have their intoxicating perils. Even when it comes to sexuality, however, it's of little use to approach digital culture as simply an enhancement of our basest purposes. If committed relationships are the inverse of casual sex, for instance, it's worth noting that online dating is a far bigger business than digital swinging. In each case, one motivating factor is likely to be the unprecedented range of options and lack of self-exposure involved. Yet it's clear enough that not everyone filling out a detailed profile on sites like Match.com is in it for instant gratification – otherwise they'd be hanging out on AdultFriendFinder instead.

There's also a more nebulous middle ground. Take the Russian service ChatRoulette. Founded in November 2009, it serves up a kind of social Russian roulette, connecting random people into live conversation via webcam and microphone. Visit the site, click it into motion, and a live feed into a strange room will pop up in a box on your screen, while – assuming you have a camera and microphone – your presence will simultaneously be beamed back. Average encounters last less than a minute, thanks to the provision of a prominent 'next' button, able instantly to spin you on to another chance encounter.

Predictably enough, nudity is a common theme within a service that's perfectly tailored for exhibitionists and voyeurs: estimates in early 2010 put as many as one in eight interactions in the 'offensive' bracket. Less predictably, though, the service has been used for everything from straightforward conversations to live musical performances, web-usage studies and celebrity appearances, matched by increasingly effective means of banning those indulging in explicit acts. My own research on the site connected me to a dozen young people around the world – including a roomful of Egyptian students, an Algerian teenager, one rude American and a sweetly bewildered German – and only involved obscenities in the case of two, apparently unrelated, Turkish men.

This pattern offers an interesting counterpoint to the 'tidal waves of porn' narrative of digital history. In the early 1990s, when the internet and web opened up for the first time to a paying public, talk of this new space being clogged by sex and pornography was commonplace. You would eventually barely be able to go online, the argument went, without being bombarded by smut drawn from the world's limitless digital arsenal.

Three decades on, the erotic apocalypse has yet to materialize. In fact, what's more remarkable is just how easy it is to use all manner of digital tools and services without ever encountering more than a hint of the illicit. Should you direct your browser or search engine towards 'sex' in any form, you'll soon have a screen bursting with porn adverts, promises and images. Unless you search for it, though, or are especially web-naive, all of the filth remains happily walled up in its ghetto. Sex and pornography may be competing for our online time and attention together with everything else, but they have not managed decisively to out-compete other digital activities.

Indeed, it's almost exactly the other way around. In 1993, during the near-prehistoric early days of the internet, *Wired* magazine boldly described sex as 'a virus that infects new technology first'. As the medium became more popular and mature, the argument went, sex – which had spread like wildfire across a virgin digital landscape – would lose its edge, due in large part to its lack of potential for sophistication.

As far as digital services and websites are concerned, this argument has proved increasingly true. As of October 2011, according to the traffic-monitoring company Alexa's rankings, sex and pornography were officially less interesting to the world than Amazon, Wikipedia, the Internet Movie Database, and dozens of other services ranging from search engines to social networking. All of these ranked far higher among the world's top websites than any pornographic or sexual service, with only one sex-related site even making the global top fifty, and that at number forty-four (it's called LiveJasmin and is, Alexa notes in its report, 'visited more frequently by males who are in the age range 18–24, have no children and browse this site from home'). Fewer than ten 'adult' sites make the top one hundred. Similarly, if you use Google's Insights analysis to gauge global search interest in both 'sex' and 'porn' between 2004 and 2011, you'll find that these beat everything from 'books' to 'music' and 'movies' – but are bested in turn by searches for 'Google', 'Facebook', 'YouTube' and 'Yahoo!', among others. Like many of us, the internet isn't quite as interested in sex as it is in itself.

This is partly because much pornographic and illicit content has moved away from the mainstream web itself towards private networks, established directly and discreetly between those wishing to share files. It's also, though, because we have learned to ask for more from our technology – and from each other – over time; and because the kind of digital 'communities' exerting an increasing influence on the world are based on more than mutual exploitation.

3.

A comparison with email is instructive here. Checking my own email spam folder, the 300-odd unsolicited messages to have arrived during the last week are fairly typical: promises of sexual potency, money off electronic products, credit cards and anti-aging products, loans in US dollars, offers of of sexual partnership and, most intriguingly of all, 'important information about your dentist'. My email account is a passive receptacle for the world's junk and nonsense – and so it pours in, for me and for everyone else too, in quantities estimated to make up over 80 per cent of the several hundred billion emails sent each year around the world.

This is precisely the bombardment predicted with glee by doomsayers at the beginning of the digital era. Its logic, however, breaks down completely as soon as I become an active – and interactive – navigator of information rather than a passive recipient. For, while I may choose at times to visit pornographic sites, porn tends at best to be a resource of limited usefulness and interest when it comes to the active enjoyment of digital media.

In fact, as both content and experience, most pornography is sufficiently boring to make it extremely poor at competing for active attention online. Something to browse, choose, use and discard, it tells us little about ourselves or other people, and almost nothing that we don't already know, beyond the bounds of taste and mechanical possibility. It is its own sterile world of clichés and repetitions: a ghetto we have almost all, if we're honest, visited at some point, but in which we have little desire to spend any more time or effort than we have to.

The metaphor of the ghetto is a telling one on several levels, for it suggests something larger about the nature of online behaviour and our best efforts to regulate it – and ourselves. Speaking in 2003 at the TED conference in California, the science writer Steven Johnson outlined the ways in which he believed the World Wide Web was itself like a city: something 'built by many people, completely controlled by no one, intricately interconnected and yet functioning as many independent parts'.

Johnson's example suggests a useful framework both for getting the most out of each other and policing our new world effectively: a new world that neither centrally imposed regulation nor any amount of generic education can tame, but that relies for its thriving on the functioning of many overlapping forms of community.

Policing in the modern sense of the word – a law-enforcement agency paid by the state, but acting in the popular interest and in concert with the population at large – first arose in the sixteenth and seventeenth centuries in the context of the challenges that expanding cities posed to law, public health and happiness alike. A legitimate and effective police force had to work with local communities, and was drawn in part from them.

As I argued above, some the greatest dangers of the darker end of human behaviour online come from its potential to fuel the abuse of minorities, while having a coarsening effect on the majority. This applies not only to sex and sexuality, but to all those behaviours that seek to harm, exploit and humiliate others. In defending ourselves and our societies against these, the best digital models echo the effective policing of urban space, combining the ethos of a community in which members look out for one another with external standards enforced from within.

In 2007, in response to the problems of abuse and dishonesty he saw damaging the experience of many digital-community members around the world, the American publisher, blogger and leading light of the free-software movement Tim O'Reilly proposed a 'bloggers' code of conduct' in seven parts, drawing in part on urban metaphors like Johnson's for inspiration.

The first six points in the code focused on bloggers taking responsibility for the content that appeared on their own websites, the issue of anonymity, and how to tackle potential sources of abuse and bullying. The seventh of O'Reilly's points, however, was a more general one, and remains one of the neatest single-sentence summaries of good 'netiquette' coined to date: 'Don't say anything online that you wouldn't say in person.'

O'Reilly was making the case for a guiding principle of civility in digital interactions, and for civility in its strict etymological sense: behaviour proper to a citizen or city-dweller, who must exist in close proximity to others. 'I believe,' he subsequently explained on his own blog, 'that civility is catching, and so is uncivility. If it's tolerated, it gets worse. There is no one blogging community, just like there is no one community in a big city . . . it's not an accident that "civil" is also the first two syllables of 'civilization'.'

This idea of treating people as if they were with you 'in person' is a powerful one. One form of online objectification just as pernicious as pornography is so-called cyber-bullying, which can range from simple verbal abuse to prolonged persecution across sites and services affecting work and leisure.

In her 2011 book *Alone Together*, the American psychologist and MIT professor Sherry Turkle paints an alarming picture of the degree to which some young lives are damaged by such behaviours. One of her interviewees, a student called Zeke, describes scanning in pictures from magazines to construct profiles for imaginary people whose identities he then uses to begin extremely critical conversations about himself on MySpace. He then sees who else among his contacts joins in as a way, he explains, 'to find out if people hate you' – an expectation that's unlikely to be disappointed, in the intensely anxious, backbiting subculture he inhabits, where digital ostracism is a form of social death.

Depersonalization, in cases like Zeke's, entails the exploitation of digital ease and unreality to hollow out the central values of a life: social identity, the ability to relate and be related to sympathetically, opportunities for honest self-expression and sharing.

Technology is an enabler, not the root cause, of all this. We are all, today, able to satisfy many of our most primitive tendencies at whim in the digital realm – and most of us will, at some point. Yet we all also need to be more than objects to each other; to find spaces both online and offline that accept us 'in person', as people to whom civility is owed.

Anonymity is not an inexorable evil, here, any more than knowing someone's name guarantees their good behaviour. What we must resist, rather, is the kind of self-interest that treats all onscreen interactions – whether anonymous, within a virtual world, or among friends on Facebook – as serving nothing beyond individual gratification. This is above all a question about the strength and integrity of our communities, and their capacities for mixing effective self-regulation with respect for shared standards: for self-policing, but knowing when recourse to authority is required. In each case, some lines must be drawn. Online and in person, we are only as human as others allow us to be.

7. Play and Pleasure

I.

In 2006, the American psychologist Geoffrey Miller used an essay in *Seed* magazine to explore the question known as Fermi's Paradox, after the Italian-American physicist Enrico Fermi, who first proposed it in the late 1950s. Why, Fermi asked, has humanity never found any evidence of intelligent alien life, given the vast size and age of the universe, and the number of potentially hospitable planets it contains?

Traditional answers to Fermi's question range from the suggestion that alien life is incredibly unlikely, to the speculation that the aliens have all blown themselves up – or they do exist and have found us, but don't want us to know. Miller, however, offers a theory that would have been unlikely to occur to Fermi himself: 'I think the aliens don't blow themselves up. They just get addicted to computer games.'

For more than a century, science fiction has explored the possibility of artificially constructed utopias: from Aldous Huxley's sinister vision of human perfection in *Brave New World* to the humanoid robots and artificially controlled emotions of Philip K. Dick's fiction. Miller, however, represents a more subtly troubling strand of utopian speculation. Rather than build a heaven on earth, he suggests, we might some day simply opt out of actuality altogether.

Increasingly, it seems that at least a diluted form of this possibility is taking place in the world around us. According to the American game designer Jane McGonigal, author of the 2010 book *Reality Is Broken*, humanity now collectively spends more than three billion hours a week on electronic games. It's a number that is only going to increase. We are seeing a mass migration of human effort, attention, relationships and identities towards artificial environments designed expressly to entertain and enthral us.

In a phrase coined by Edward Castronova, an American economist and researcher into virtual worlds, the relationship between virtual activities and someone's life-satisfaction can confront them with a 'toxic immersion dilemma': a conflict between the very real pleasures afforded by immersion in a virtual space, and the potentially toxic effect of this immersion on their life and their society as a whole.

In August 2011, Castronova and the German economics professor Gert G. Wagner published a study entitled 'Virtual Life Satisfaction' in the journal *Kyklos*. The study compared data from the 2005 World Values Survey with a 2009 survey of users of the virtual world Second Life, contrasting the relative changes in life-satisfaction caused by life events such as unemployment and by participation in the virtual world.

The most striking aspect of Castronova and Wagner's results was not that using Second Life enhanced life-satisfaction – something you would expect, given that its entire point is to entertain. Rather, it was the *size* of the increase in life-satisfaction associated with playing it. Within academic studies of happiness, the correlation between being unemployed and having low life-satisfaction is one of the strongest results to be found. The chunk of life-satisfaction gained by playing Second Life, however, was almost equal to that gained by finding a job and thus ceasing to be unemployed.

'This,' the authors noted, 'leads to some interesting speculations ... Given that "moving" to Second Life involves little more than a computer and an internet connection (and free time, which the unemployed have in abundance), the comparable effect sizes here suggest that some people may be strongly motivated to take refuge in a virtual life rather than try to change their real life.'

The implications of the study are double-edged. On the one hand, it emphasizes the fact that for users of virtual environments, the time they spend in them often pays off richly in terms of emotional rewards. On the other hand, it returns us to real life's limitations as a source of satisfaction when contrasted with simulated environments – and to the question of whether we should be aiming to improve the real world, intervene against the seductions of virtual ones, or both.

2.

The concept of 'play' is an emblem of much of our digitally mediated lives – and of the deep-seated pleasure we take in being able to exit, temporarily, life's unbounded problems, for arenas offering certainty and resolution. When I look at many of the world's most success-ful online services, from YouTube to Twitter to Facebook, I'm always struck by just how like a game they are: rewarding users' efforts with metrics like the number of friends or contacts or messages; creating a steady, engaging flow of actions and reactions, complete with oppor-tunities for co-operation and competition. Sometimes, of course, we need to grow up. But the allure of these playful mechanisms will remain. And it suggests, to my mind, the extent to which digital play offers a window into the evolving future of our wants and behaviours – and how the playful freedom of these spaces may reshape what we expect both of our societies and each other.

One intriguing concept within all this is 'playbour' – a word combining 'play' and 'labour' that describes the expanding economy of real labour devoted to goods that only exist within virtual worlds.

The very word 'exist' can seem a problematic one here. Both my wife and I have played the online fantasy game World of Warcraft since its launch in 2004. Our in-game characters represent many thousands of hours of effort, and the equipment they carry has been earned through weeks' worth of adventuring, exploration and daring assaults in the company of dozens of other players. In what sense, though, do these pixilated avatars 'exist', given that their presence in the world amounts to little more than an electrical charge on a disk within the computer system of the company that operates the game?

The only meaningful answer to this question is one that invokes collective belief. The value of my World of Warcraft character is no more or less real than the value of the money in my bank account – or rather, it is similarly contingent on faith and consensus. Over ten million people around the world have paid for the right to play World of Warcraft. If one of these players in America wishes to get some amazing equipment for his character without having to invest hundreds of hours in the game, someone else's efforts become worth precisely what he or she is prepared to pay them; a going rate that, at its peak, could amount to over a thousand US dollars for an exceptional character.

The industry serving this kind of need is largely not sanctioned by games companies, yet it is worth hundreds of millions of dollars

– testimony to the scale of the belief, time and effort now invested in virtual environments. And, despite the bizarre disjunct evoked by paying hundreds or even thousands of dollars for a virtual artefact (the current record for a virtual goods sale was set in 2010 by a space station in the game Entropia Universe, which sold for $330,000), this makes a certain kind of sense, given the emotional experiences the best games offer people prepared to 'work' hard at playing them.

It's no coincidence, for example, that many of the world's most popular game worlds invoke pastoral simplicities – farms, medieval castles, idealized grassy landscapes – or that a hard day's play within them revolves around crop harvesting or trade skills, minus the gruelling bother of back-breaking labour. From the creation of products we can be proud of to the pleasures of successful collaboration around a common challenge, certain emotional satisfactions are not on offer in many working lives in the real world. By contrast, the idyllic simplicity of skilled effort being immediately rewarded by a useful and attractive result – even a virtual one – can be as satisfying in its way as crafting a wooden bowl or baking a loaf of bread.

I'm not someone who spends – or earns – hard currency in virtual worlds, beyond my monthly subscription to several. Yet I find it difficult to draw a firm distinction between a friend spending £50 on a pair of labelled jeans and their using that money instead to buy their in-game avatar a virtual designer outfit. One is tangible, the other digital. Neither, though, is necessary – and the virtual version may well get more use and give more hours of pleasure.

The same fundamental economics governs each of these purchases, rooted not in any inherent value, but in the position these

Players too busy, or impatient, to advance in a game themselves can even outsource it to China, where people will play for you – at a price.

objects occupy in various networks of scarcity, perception, information and display. The very description of an object as 'virtual' can be
misleading in such a context. For as we begin to take it for granted
that owning data and pixels can be every bit as serious a business as
trading oil, regulating unreal transactions becomes an increasingly
real concern – not least because of the novel ways in which such
objects are created, owned and earned. Where collective belief is king,
only an economic structure that truly inspires the confidence of its
users will survive – something that may end up making virtual assets
a more appealing investment than many supposedly 'real' ones.

3.

When it comes to unreality, immersion in ersatz medieval labour is
no longer the only game in town. In the 1980s and 1990s, it seemed
that the most thrilling future for digital entertainment lay in immer-
sive virtual worlds. Yet just over a decade on, it's becoming increasingly clear that the future of online pleasure may look less like *The
Matrix* than something at once simpler and broader in its reach.

As I have mentioned, World of Warcraft, the most lucrative
online role-playing game in history, has attracted around ten million
paying subscribers in the seven years since its launch. Since its
release in December 2009, by comparison, a very different species
of game has successfully jacked itself into the lives of more than half
a billion users: Angry Birds.

Angry Birds is a game of almost elemental simplicity. In a cute,
two-dimensional cartoon world, naughty pigs have stolen some eggs

from the eponymous birds. Your task is to help the birds recover these by demolishing several hundred screens' worth of the pigs' rickety fortifications, in each case by launching catapult shots from a fixed location.

It's what is known as a 'physics-based game', because the fun comes from carefully picking the angle and power of a limited number of shots intended to demolish the fortifications and splat the pigs. Aside from a few different types of bird – which act as your ammunition – that is a complete summary of the game. Using a touch-screen device, such as a smartphone or tablet, you pull back the catapult elastic with your finger, aim, and release. And repeat. Many thousands of times.

Angry Birds is a child of the latest phase in the development of game-playing technology: the rise of powerful mobile computing devices in the form of smartphones and tablets. Almost overnight, electronic gaming has ceased to be the preserve of self-designated 'gamers' playing on expensive consoles or computers. Instead, electronic play is fast becoming a universal pastime.

On a commute, waiting for a meeting, even standing in a lift or on an escalator, casual games like Angry Birds allow the injection of an intensely absorbing kind of fun into even a handful of free minutes. They banish boredom; they demand skill and reward effort. They do, in fact, everything Geoffrey Miller was writing about in 2006 when he imagined aliens chasing 'shiny pennies of pleasure' rather than searching for other life in the universe. Whether it's Angry Birds or Warcraft, the psychological mechanisms that make for a good game are similar, at root, to those that make for most kinds of good digital experience.

They involve a limited, bounded arena where the open-ended complexity of actuality is replaced by something simpler and more intense: a series of problems to be solved, or actions to be performed, guaranteed to work out if done correctly. In this sense, Angry Birds is indeed a utopia: an unchanging Eden of grass, blue skies, birds and pigs within which every single player can eventually master every single level – and where learning to do so is a largely delightful process.

In sociological terms, Angry Birds presents what is known as a 'tame' problem. First addressed in a 1973 treatise by the social theorists Horst Rittel and Melvin Webber, tame problems include games like chess and the majority of mathematical propositions. They are problems in which the person trying to solve them has all the necessary data at their disposal, and knows from the beginning that there is a final solution or winning proposition.

In contrast to these are 'wicked' problems: problems where there is no way of formulating the issue at stake definitively, nor any such thing as a single or definitive solution. Each wicked problem is a unique set of circumstances, themselves entwined with other sets of problems. A typical wicked problem might be the economic health of a country or company, or somebody trying to decide the best course of action in their personal life. In each case, the only kind of solution that can be hoped for is a strategy that 'tames' aspects of the problem, breaking it into different elements and suggesting better and worse ways of tackling these.

In these terms, life itself is a wicked problem. In one of science fiction's greatest jokes, Douglas Adams imagined, in the *Hitchhiker's Guide to the Galaxy* books, a supercomputer providing the

'Ultimate Answer to the Ultimate Question of Life, The Universe, and Everything': a single number, 42. The joke rests on the absurd mismatch between the kind of problem that can be answered by one number and the very different kind of 'problem' that life represents. The very idea that life (let alone the Universe or Everything) has an answer in the way that a game of chess of Angry Birds does is a delightful nonsense.

In play, we abandon the wicked for the tame. This is a deep part of why play pleases us so much; and why, in evolutionary terms, it has so much importance across the animal kingdom. Play is a safe state within which we learn skills, from co-ordination and combat to speed and concealment. We play in order to practise for life – because life itself is never practice. In the real world, moments and opportunities come only once – 'the unbearable lightness of being' in the Czech author Milan Kundera's phrase.

4.

Predictability and repeatability are among the greatest joys of the digital realm. Everyone can be the hero of their own story, and can experience progress and success. Those who are bored or alienated can boost their life-satisfaction with an ease that reality cannot match – or can take refuge from unbearable circumstances.

Writing in the *Guardian* in November 2008, the British novelist Naomi Alderman described how, living in Manhattan in 2001, she used video games to escape a real world that had temporarily become unbearably loaded with anxiety following the 9/11 terrorist attacks.

Alderman's game of choice was Diablo II. Set in a fantasy world of demons and undead legions, you play as a heroic character and can team up with friends in order to vanquish near-endless dungeons full of enemies. 'I remember surfacing from four-hour Diablo II sessions feeling as if I'd been on holiday,' she recalled, 'so grateful that I'd been able to blot out the images of genuine horror filling my city. The game was so mind-filling it left no room for the anxious brooding that I was experiencing the rest of the time. This was a tremendous blessing.'

Within game worlds like Diablo II – indeed, within the confines of any well-designed digital service – some of the wickedest problems of living can at least temporarily be supplanted by a tamer species of experience. Moreover, as writers and theorists like Jane McGonigal have argued, this principle can be taken one stage further, in using the lessons of the best games and technologies to make reality itself 'better'. That is, we can attempt to refine worldly processes of reward, engagement, education and teamwork in the light of new technology and its rich seams of behavioural data: a process sometimes summarized by the dismayingly ugly term 'gamification'.

One simple example is domestic power consumption: a distinctly unglamorous topic, but an important component in most proposals for lowering global carbon emissions. There's good evidence that replacing a standard electricity meter with one showing consumption in real time makes people more aware of the energy being used by different domestic devices. Some game designers and psychologists are interested in taking this kind of feedback much further, using expertise gained from the business of building engaging games.

Setting people varied tasks and targets over time, for example, can aid long-term motivation and engagement; as can sharing data and feedback with neighbours or neighbourhoods, encouraging others to try harder or adopt better strategies. Then there are larger possibilities, such as awarding points for various kinds of effort and achievement, and connecting these to redeemable rewards, leaderboards, and educational and reference systems. As Mark Twain's Tom Sawyer knew back in 1876, you can turn even painting a fence into an engaging experience if you can make mastering it feel like a special achievement.

In each case, the psychological lessons are nothing inherently new. What is new, however, is the degree of sophistication and automation digital technologies can bring to bear on these insights, and the practical examples that can be taken from the world's most successful digital games and services.

These kinds of lesson are not applicable to every situation. Yet in them we can, I believe, see the shape of a productive dialogue between the best digital techniques for engagement, and bettering engagement in issues ranging from education to environmental awareness and political participation. When it comes to learning, in particular, we are already beginning to see in the habits and skills of the emerging generation of 'digital natives' how lessons drawn from games may, in time, transform both the inclusiveness and the effectiveness of education systems.

As a species, we evolved over hundreds of thousands of years to find certain things satisfying. Today, we have begun to engage in an extraordinary kind of reverse engineering: building artificial worlds and spaces designed to intrigue and delight us, free from nature's complexities and disappointments. The amplification of our species' potential promised by this process is incredible. Together, we are almost immeasurably more now than we have ever been. Individually, we have a scope inconceivable a century ago.

Yet in our potency, we are vulnerable; and we cannot afford to lose sight of the fact that no complete solutions for living exist in the tame realm of our own creations. Perfection of a kind is possible in a game like Angry Birds. Given enough time and effort, every single one of the world's hundreds of millions of users can earn three out of three stars on every single level. We do not and cannot have this in the real world; and we are in trouble if we learn to expect it, or fail to develop strategies for coping with life's wicked, unrewarded, one-time sorrows.

8. The New Politics

I.

What do the Tea Party movement in the US, the anti-copyright Pirate Party founded in Scandinavia, the events of the Arab Spring and the global protest group Occupy have in common? There's little ideological common ground between them, to say the least. All, however, represent a new kind of politics that has emerged over the last few decades: one predicated on the viral spread of ideas and ideologies, and on forms of political action conducted more like franchises than traditional, top-down party operations.

To take part, all you need to do is check off the ideological touchstones, deploy digital and conventional means to organize your action, and launch it under the banner of the movement. There may be leaders, but there is no single chain of command. It's usually far clearer what the movement hates and opposes than what, exactly, it proposes the world do differently. And unless those in authority are prepared to exert brutal force in response – as has proved the case in parts of the Middle East – the consequences may be transforming, even revolutionary.

In a metaphor coined by the British writer and philosopher Ren Reynolds, these political trends are like waves in a river – while the substance that allows them to exist, the flowing water itself, is the new politics of a digitally interconnected age.

For as we become more connected, we are beginning to approach politics in new ways. Official party memberships and voting turn-outs have fallen consistently across most developed democracies over the last half-century. Proclaimed trust in politicians is close to an all-time low, while the traditional custodians of public political debate – newspapers and broadcasters – are faring little better in public affections or interest. Consult the news headlines, though, and you'll find it difficult not to come across political actions involv-ing remarkable numbers of disparate people: global protests railing against a particular injustice; darker organizations sowing terror and dissent.

At the time of writing, in late 2011, New York and London were both experiencing city-centre occupations by the anti-corporate protest movement Occupy – a movement that, thanks to old and new media coverage alike, was simultaneously being imitated in over 900 other cities across the world, in nations from Honduras and Bolivia to Germany, Japan, Serbia and India. According to the 'Principles of solidarity – working draft' listed on the voluminous website of the original US occupation, this movement is 'daring to imagine a new socio-political and economic alternative that offers greater possibility of equality'.

The site also offers a 'quick guide to starting a General Assembly' for those interested in doing the same elsewhere. It's an earnestness that's easily mocked; yet the passion and quantities of comment, debate and practical expertise in evidence offer a sobering compari-son to the dearth of such popular, positive input around most issues in mainstream politics. Not for nothing did *Time* magazine declare 'the protestor' its person of the year for 2011, 'for combining the

Occupy Seattle: another ripple in the surface of the world's shifting political order.

oldest of techniques with the newest of technologies . . . for steering the planet on a more democratic though sometimes more dangerous path for the 21st century'.

As in other fields, the boundaries around different kinds of political experience have been fundamentally shifted by new technology. For twenty-first-century citizens, able digitally both to access and participate in groups of many thousands or even millions, 'politics' is not so much a selection of discrete acts as part of the daily ebb and flow of living. Whether we are aware of our participation or not is largely beside the point: ignorance has its politics as surely as activism does. As everything from local government to taxation, voting and personal data moves steadily towards global digital networks, the stakes for both action and inertia are also steadily increasing.

2.

Ever since the commercial opening-up of the internet and the creation of the web in 1989, digital media have moved steadily from simply reporting the politics of our time to actively helping to create them. Today, from global protest politics to the impact of Wikileaks and the global hackers' collective Anonymous, old balances of power are shifting with remarkable speed away from those minorities who have throughout most of history monopolized knowledge and organizational tools.

Yet the seductive belief that access to the internet can simply be equated with democratic freedom does little justice to the complexities of this situation. To pick only the most obvious exception, China boasts both the world's largest online population – over 300 million users and counting – and its most sophisticated regime of monitoring, censorship and espionage. Digital tools can aid many freedoms; but their story is far from simple, and far from likely to end in either revolution or wholesale reform.

In all this, perhaps the greatest danger is not apathy but naivety: the failure to grasp fully the potentials and pitfalls of the tools at our disposal. Consider privacy and online security. The simple fact that each one of us now leaves behind a series of digital footprints visible for all eternity poses profound legislative and ethical questions – and ones that most nation states remain many years behind in addressing.

What does and should privacy mean online – and how much control should we be able to exert over information of all kinds once we have sent it out into the world? This is a political question that many legislators and citizens alike are ill equipped to answer. The idea that we have 'rights' in a digital space, as both consumers and citizens, is still barely enshrined in law beyond definitions of the most blatant kinds of criminality; and extending existing legal models into the kind of trans-national spaces created by the internet is extremely tricky, especially when it comes to the ownership and safeguarding of properties whose physical reality is as mere particles in an electronic data cloud.

Any comprehensive legislation will be many years – if not decades – in the making. In the meantime, the onus is overwhelmingly on ordinary users and corporate interests to negotiate the basis on which personal information can be held safely in ever-greater quantities. Furthermore, we must consider the criteria by which our larger actions in digital spaces, from social networking messages to emails and uploads, will be judged and held legally accountable.

What isn't in doubt is just how politically real these issues have already become. Following rioting across the UK in August 2011, two men who separately used messages on Facebook to incite rioting in Northwich Town were sentenced to four years in prison each, despite no one actually attending any event as a result or causing any physical damage. They had, the judge noted, caused 'panic and revulsion in local communities as rumours of anticipated violence spread' – a curious mirror image of the more familiar story of 'good' anti-government protestors elsewhere being jailed for their attempts to organize political actions or spread information.

3.

It's clear that we need to grow up fast when it comes to debating digital politics – not least in determining where the truly important questions lie. As the author Evgeny Morozov notes in his 2011 book *The Net Delusion*, 'the technological visionaries we count on to guide us into a brighter digital future may excel at solving the wrong kind of problem . . . . Since the only hammer such visionaries have is the internet, it's not surprising that every possible social and political problem is presented as an online nail.' Morozov's point is an important one: if there is hope, it lies in examining technology not in isolation, but rather as a part of the particular social and cultural arenas in which it operates.

Is Big Brother watching you – and your Facebook account?

When it comes to the direct impact of new technologies on politics itself, we must first ask what, exactly, the new kind of political acts permitted by digital networks are – and which old ones are either being facilitated to a new degree, or rendered increasingly irrelevant.

Three factors are crucial here: the capacity of individuals to document what is taking place around them and what they believe; the ease with which such documents can be shared and broadcast; and the related ease of rapidly organizing massed forms of action that can themselves be documented and communicated. This was, in essence, the pattern of activity that defined the beginnings of the Arab Spring uprisings in Tunisia and Egypt – a pattern characterized not so much by its unimpeachable moral standing as by its novelty and effectiveness in regions for so long so tightly controlled.

Even if these technologies and trends do favour citizens over central authorities, though, how can we tell which 'online nails', in Morozov's terms, represent merely wishful thinking, and where government budgets and individual efforts can best be spent?

One of the most significant global thinkers in this field is the American academic Tim Wu. The usual story of media, Wu argues in his 2010 book *The Master Switch*, is of a journey from openness to monopoly. At the start of the twentieth century, the birth of radio fuelled hopes in America and elsewhere that this technology would usher in an era of unprecedented democratic participation. Yet what actually happened through the 1920s and 1930s was the transition of radio from 'a wide-open medium' to a 'big business, dominated by a Radio Trust': an economic closing-down of possibilities that did more to restrict freedom of expression via this fledgling medium than any government agenda.

When it comes to the internet, Wu argues that something different is going on than in the cases of print, television or radio. The internet's unique design – whose 'priority was human augmentation rather than the system itself' – means that what was created was 'a decentralized network, and one that would stay that way'. Yet 'political command and control of the internet' is not impossible – it is simply far harder than for other media.

Authoritarian regimes, if they know what they're doing, may indeed muster enough force to overcome most digital protest, or the opportunities for it. Similarly, sufficiently misguided legislation or malicious corporate practice may derail many of the open internet's current virtues; or drive consumers seeking safety and convenience straight into the hands of censors and monopolies. It all depends on how alert we – and those we elect, or those we pay for the privilege of digital access – are to such possibilities.

'The internet,' Wu concludes,

> is simply not the infinitely elastic phantasm that it is popularly imagined to be, but rather an actual physical entity that can be warped or broken. For while the network is designed to connect every user with every other on an equal footing, it has always depended on a finite number of physical connections, whether wired or spectral, and switches, operated by a finite number of firms upon whose good behaviour the whole thing depends.

The sooner we take on board the full consequences of this the better. The open structures underpinning digital culture often interact uneasily with existing systems of politics and commerce – and the best results, for both individuals and the world, are only likely to emerge from a negotiation which all players are able to fight their corners with equal force and knowledge.

Perhaps most significantly in global terms, however, the fruits of this process may be reaped not chiefly by the wealthy or the current elite, but by those people and nations who have not historically been at the forefront of development. As the recent uprisings in the Middle East and North Africa suggest, many of those most fervently embracing the digital age's possibilities are not its pioneers, but those who stand to gain the most from the chance to leapfrog a technological generation.

Take the case of India: a country in which there is no equivalent of the American social security system or British National Insurance, and where out of a population of 1.2 billion people only 33 million pay income tax, and only 60 million have passports. As the *New Yorker* magazine reported in October 2011, 'hundreds of millions of Indians are barely visible to the state . . . they can't easily open bank accounts or buy cell-phone SIM cards, and they can't secure state services owed to them'.

This is something the Indian government is trying to change via a massive digital initiative whose aim is to assign every single person in India a randomly selected, unique twelve-digit number, linked to biometric data: a photograph, fingerprints and scans of the eye.

Heading up this initiative is one Nandan Nilekani: the founder, in 1981, of the Indian software company Infosys, today worth nearly thirty billion dollars. Nilekani's initiative has proved controversial, to say the least, with national concerns being raised over everything from funding and reliability to personal security, feasibility, and the scheme's relationship to other national identification programmes.

With the scheme officially mandated to have enrolled 200 million people by March 2012, its long-term expansion remains in the balance at the time of writing. On offer, potentially, lies a new kind of relationship with the state for hundreds of millions of Indians, predicated on the basic principle of a verified identity and the social stake that comes with it. Around this, though, lurk concerns of what such a scheme might also mean: from a massive waste of resources to a curtailment of civil liberties.

4.

Looking at the ways in which digital technologies are being put to transformative use across the developing world, Nilekani's aspirations – and the difficulties surrounding them – echo a familiar pattern. On offer are new forms of participation and access for many millions of people; while the hazards that attend them flow from the new leverage that a corrupt, cynical or dangerously incompetent few might wield via new systems.

For all this, there is already much to celebrate – and much of it astonishing in both the speed and scale of change. Banking systems based on mobile-phone accounts are becoming commonplace today in South and Central America, as are methods for paying tax and even for voting via mobiles. Farming and trade are being radically altered by mobile access to pricing and market information.

To take just one example, mobile-phone access in Bangladesh – a country which until 1999 boasted no modern mobile networks – was by 2010 considered to have reached 100 per cent 'virtual' penetration, meaning that almost no Bangladeshis lived without access to mobile communications via family, friends or community. In Africa, meanwhile, there are now over six hundred million mobile-phone users: more than in either America or Europe.

Digital technology, here, is nimble and wonderfully fit for purpose in its combination of power and flexibility, and its ease of integration with even the most basic of living conditions and needs. This is the very opposite of the luxury, self-indulgence and alienation too often associated with the political impact of new technologies in the developed world: a phenomenon whose politics is rooted at the bottom of society rather than imposed from above, and that is all the more vigorous for it.

With technology playing an increasingly central global role in the disruption of established notions of what is and isn't 'political', it is far from naive to hope that new forms of political participation and integration may arise alongside new forms of connection and identity. Moreover, in the open structures underpinning much of this technology, we have a young, unique legacy to build upon and bequeath.

Much like the traditional political arena, those digital spaces within which new forms of political and social contract are being forged are themselves sure to be endlessly fraught with conflicts, negotiations and compromises. To thrive together, we must be prepared to stand up for our freedoms within these spaces: freedom of expression and protest; equality and openness of access; personal privacy and ownership of information.

In all these areas, there's an urgent need for good legislation and regulation. In the end, however, the forces shaping our political future are at once fluid and highly devolved: distributed as never before between overlapping communities, movements and interests. Single, centralized solutions will not save or safeguard us. New bargains are there to be struck, and new forms of inclusiveness ripe to be explored: but only if all sides are able to muster enough knowledge, ambition and faith in each others' capacities for action.

Conclusion

I have traced eight interwoven strands of argument in this book, moving outwards from individual experiences of time, attention and sharing to the structures that surround these: the cultural, political and ethical values implicated in the emerging facts of digital technology. And I have offered what I hope are useful conclusions about what it means to thrive within these areas.

We must, I believe, look to the nature of our experiences rather than the tools creating them if we hope to understand the present. We must cherish the best of these experiences – but also carve out a space apart from technology in our lives, and take control of our attention, apportioning our time knowingly rather than allowing always-on devices to dictate the texture of every moment. This means finding a balance within our habits both of thought and of action – and believing that it is possible to assert different ways of thinking and being against the pressures of constant connection.

We must, too, understand something of the histories of the digital tools and services we use, and critique them as we do other human creations, rather than inhabiting them like a landscape. We must learn not simply to share, but to share well – and to participate in the digital commons with the kind of integrity that breeds integrity in others. And we must try harder than ever to find times and means of being entirely ourselves; of drawing on the riches of present and past culture, and escaping the pressures of received wisdom and group response.

The digital tools we possess make many different kinds of action seem easy and free of consequence. We are freer than ever to use and abuse others, or at least their digital shadows; to indulge prejudice and untruth; to exist merely reflexively in every field from sexuality to work or creativity.

This kind of freedom has its siren call; yet it is not the only future I see being built online, or embodied in the deep architecture of a digital era. For all its flaws and local abuses, the world now possesses an unprecedentedly open and equal system of information-sharing and mass opportunity. No one nation or organization has the ability to control this yet, just as no one service or trend – no matter how potent its appeal or lobbyists – has yet managed to colonize our every digital experience.

Preserving and negotiating the future of this openness is a task for everyone, and one that demands new kinds of relationships between governments, citizens, corporations and associations of members. Not all stakes are equal. In some places, the deck is already grotesquely stacked. Yet many of the great opportunities are only just beginning to emerge.

Although they can serve as an indulgence for the privileged, digital technologies are already proving an engine of extraordinary change for those who have least: passage for the first time into membership of and participation in nation states, commerce, and the wider realms of culture, innovation and ideas.

Comprehending and regulating this communal arena is a challenge as great as any in human history, one in which billions rather than millions of actors are both implicated and, increasingly, embodied. Yet in this, as in so much, our greatest problems and our most hopeful answers are pinned together: in online communities, repositories of expertise and guidance, and inspirational precedents across the world. Our digital selves may be uniquely vulnerable, but we are also rarely more than a click away from something or someone that might help us – if we know how to look and who to ask.

Finally, there is the question of our own natures – and where our new capacities for self-delight and distraction may lead us. Technology can be a delight and a path towards action in the world; but it also has the potential to unbalance both individual lives and the societies around them. To engage productively with this dichotomy, we must differentiate between the tame, bounded arena of digital freedom and the often inchoate problems life itself throws at us. The one cannot substitute for, or fully teach us how to succeed at, the other. Yet we can, I believe, learn much about how to tame at least some segments of our world, and to better to engage today's and tomorrow's citizens.

All of these arguments and beliefs are rooted in a humanist perspective – as I believe all questions of what it means to thrive must be. We are the only measure of our own success; and this is not a metric that can be definitively qualified.

Over two millennia ago, Aristotle used the concept of *eudaimonia* to describe human thriving or flourishing. Rather than material success or physical pleasure, *eudaimonia* means living in the fullest

The School of Athens: lasting lessons on living a balanced life, and not an iPad in sight.

possible human sense. Etymologically, the term is drawn from two words meaning 'good' and a 'guardian spirit', and it implies a state similar to being watched over by a divine spirit.

When it came to determining the nature of *eudaimonia*, Aristotle turned to another, related concept: *areté*, meaning virtue or excellence. To be the best a human could be meant achieving excellence in the highest forms of human endeavour. And these, Aristotle argued, were the fields of virtue and reason: those faculties unique to human beings among all of creation.

The life of virtuous contemplation, today, may be unlikely to prove a satisfying – or feasible – answer to the question of thriving for most people. Yet it seems clear, looking at the current and future state of technology, that our most remarkable achievements and potentials still lie in the mental realm; and that any kind of excellence in this area is closely bound to our faculties of both reason and virtue.

Saying that we are the only measure of our own success can also be put another way: that we are the only measures of each others' success. Much like words, our individual identities have little meaning without context. We negotiate and renegotiate our selves constantly.

Today, that process is taking on a whole new character in the shifting collectives of the digital world. Reason – one of those attributes Aristotle claimed for humanity alone – is now a property of our tools, too: machines of ever-increasing complexity that we have made, and that are helping to remake us in turn. Yet we need not be diminished by this process. Rather, we should be driven still further in asking what it is that makes us uniquely human, and that binds us to each other.

As the American author Brian Christian – an author well steeped in Aristotle – puts it in his 2011 book, *The Most Human Human*, 'if there's one thing I think the human race has been guilty of for a long time – since antiquity at least – it's a kind of complacency, a kind of entitlement'. This entitlement is above all an intellectual one: a sense of our minds' uniqueness, and their unchallenged special status in the universe.

Today, we are challenged as we have never been before. We are challenged by the lightning logic and infinite capacities of machines; by the digital presence of several billion humans; by a billion times that quantity again of data; and by what this implies for our own sense of uniqueness and agency. Yet we also face opportunities for both action and insight that should be the envy of history.

Thriving means rising to these challenges. Are we up to the task? Not all of us, and not all of the time. Today, in an age of unfolding and unprecedented interconnections, both the prizes and the price of failure are higher than ever. Above all, then, we must begin – turn on, boot up and tune in – and find out together what we can become.

Homework

Technology shifts so fast that it can be hard to know where to turn for lasting insights. These authors and resources have collectively provided much of the intellectual impetus behind this book – and I hope they will inspire you, too.

Introduction

'The Machine Stops', E.M. Forster's 1909 short story, remains one of the most delicately moving imaginings of what future technologies may mean for humanity (*Collected Stories*, Penguin, 2001).

First published in 1934, Lewis Mumford's *Technics and Civilization* (University of Chicago, 2010) was the first true work of technological philosophy, and remains an important milestone in the history of examining how technologies transform us as we use them.

What Technology Wants by Kevin Kelly (Viking, 2010) is a wide-ranging, provocative book based on the unusual device of personifying technology and asking what it 'wants' us to do.

The glossy in-house bible of technological modernity, *Wired* magazine, is an essential stop for the look and feel of the future as geeks would love to know it.

If you want to experience a vision of the digital future in the flesh, drop into the Apple stores in London or New York, and watch the adoring shoppers' faces.

1. From Past to Present

David Leavitt's biography of Alan Turing, *The Man Who Knew Too Much* (Phoenix, 2007), is a useful account of computing's founding genius and the historical context of his work – and of the appalling sadness of Turing's later life.

Some knowledge of both maths and philosophy is vital for grasping many technological ideas; a charming introduction to both can be found in Apostolos Doxiadis and Christos H. Papadimitriou's graphic novel *Logicomix* (Bloomsbury, 2009).

Marshall McLuhan's *Understanding Media* (Routledge, 2001), first published in 1964, remains an influential and prophetic account of what media suffusion means for modern lives.

Weaving The Web (Orion, 1999) by Tim Berners-Lee – the inventor of the World Wide Web – offers a definitive history of how much of the digital world came to be as it is.

Snow Crash (Penguin), Neal Stephenson's third novel, appeared in 1992, and its imagining of possible cybernetic futures has had real influence on subsequent thinking.

Of all future-focused recent films, *Minority Report* contains arguably the most compelling and completely imagined backdrop of our imminent future.

2. Wired and Unwired Time

For lasting wisdom pertinent to our creations' impact on our lives, Plato's writings – composed when writing itself was a relatively young technology – are always worth revisiting, and *Phaedrus* in particular.

The first volume of Anthony Kenny's *New History of Western Philosophy* (OUP, 2010) also offers a wise, succinct summary of Plato's work and his era.

The Case for Working with Your Hands by Matthew Crawford (Viking, 2010) is a heartfelt counterbalance to contemporary affection for complex machines.

In *The Nature of Technology* (Penguin, 2010), W. Brian Arthur goes back to basics on what technology can – and cannot – do for us, and what is driving it onwards.

The Shallows by Nicholas Carr (Atlantic, 2011) makes the case for the values of offline reading, and the joys of deeply felt time spent away from digital devices.

Among the world's wittiest critiques of all things digital can be found in the web-comics at xkcd.com – essential chortling for geeks wanting to think outside the box.

3. Taking Control

Alone Together by Sherry Turkle (Basic Books, 2011) offers a closely observed account of the impact of emerging technologies on daily living and our relations with each other.

One of the twentieth century's finest articulations of rational scepticism, Carl Sagan's *The Demon-Haunted World* (Headline, 1997) is a perfect guide to human vulnerabilities.

John Locke's *An Essay Concerning Human Understanding* (Oxford University Press, 2008) – cited in this chapter – remains a brilliant exposition of the nature of thought. Chapter nineteen, 'Of the Modes of Thinking', is particularly relevant to this book.

Online, the site Lifehacker.com is bursting with advice on how to 'hack' your own life and achieve productivity and focus.

For those hoping to recover a sense of reverie in their lives, the essays of Montaigne remain among history's finest accounts of the unconstrained life of the mind.

If you want to take control of your own writing life, trying downloading a free application like Dark Room, which shuts down all onscreen stimulations other than pure typing.

For a digital antidote to shallowness, visit the free online archive of the *Paris Review*'s interviews with authors from T.S. Eliot to Umberto Eco at www.theparisreview.org/interviews.

4. Reframing Technology

Through the lives of four eminent Victorians, *The Philosophical Breakfast Club* by Laura J. Snyder (Broadway Books, 2011) provides rich context for the development of modern scientific culture as we know it.

A history of media and monopolies through the twentieth century, *The Master Switch* by Tim Wu (Atlantic, 2011) makes a detailed case for the importance of open, accountable media structures.

Googled by Ken Auletta (Penguin, 2009) and *The Facebook Effect* by David Kirkpatrick (Simon & Schuster, 2010) tell, in insiders' detail, the stories of two of the most important corporations of the last decade.

Walter Isaacson's biography of Apple's late CEO Steve Jobs (Little, Brown, 2011) offers at times chilling insights into the life of one of the driving forces behind the digital present.

One of the world's finest online cornucopias of both pop-cultural artefacts and home-grown technological forms is the blog BoingBoing.net

Use the web to bring history to your desktop with Oxford's remarkable Early Manuscripts service at image.ox.ac.uk – offering exquisitely detailed free scans of hundreds of ancient documents.

5. Sharing, Expertise and the End of Authority

Two books mentioned in this chapter – Robert Levine's *Free Ride* (Bodley Head, 2011) and Andrew Keen's *The Cult of the Amateur* (Nicholas Brealey, 2007) – provocatively anatomize the darker side of the economic and intellectual consequences of the internet.

A more positive view of sharing and digital potentials can be found in Clay Shirky's books in praise of the new media order, *Here Comes Everybody* (Allen Lane, 2008) and *Cognitive Surplus* (Allen Lane, 2010).

Perhaps the best book written about why it isn't all intellectual doom, gloom and dumbing-down online is Steven Johnson's *Everything Bad is Good for You* (Penguin, 2006).

Convergence Culture by Henry Jenkins (New York University Press, 2006) remains one of the classic texts exploring the consequences of new media for culture both high and low.

For those who like their online reading philosophically literate and debated in detail, the blog CrookedTimber.org is one of the best.

A perfect demonstration of how the web can do high-intellectual culture proud, the Philosophy Bites Podcast at www.philosophybites.com offers hundreds of free-to-listen interviews with the world's greatest living thinkers.

6. On Becoming Less than Human

For an eloquently provocative view on pornography and the future of sex, *Pornoland* (Thames and Hudson, 2004) – a handsome hardback with a text by Martin Amis and photography by Stefano De Luigi – delves deeply into contemporary obsessions.

Another classic of erotic reportage with plenty of insights for the present is David Foster Wallace's essay 'Big Red Son', collected in *Consider The Lobster* (Abacus, 2007).

In fiction, Iain M. Banks's 'Culture' novels – from *Consider Phlebas* (Orbit, 1988) to *Surface Detail* (Orbit, 2010) – are both a cut above the ordinary SF fare, and radical in their imaginings of the possible sexual behaviours of a sufficiently advanced society.

The 2008 Byron Review commissioned by the British government under the title 'Safer Children in a Digital World' offers a pragmatic, evidence-based assessment of the dangers and myths surrounding digital youth culture. It can be downloaded for free via the Department of Education website at: www.education.gov.uk/publications/standard/publicationdetail/page1/DCSF-00334-2008

For personal freedom and novel forms of flirtation, the classic virtual environment Second Life remains worth both exploring and reading about. Tim Guest's *Second Lives* (Arrow, 2008) is a good place to start.

7. Play and Pleasure

Play Money by Julian Dibbell (Basic Books, 2006) is one of the more unusual books on virtual worlds to have appeared: the thoughtfully told story of how the author spent a year living entirely by buying and selling virtual items for real money.

Greg Bear's novel *City at the End of Time* (Gollancz, 2008) is a rich, troubling fantasy exploring possible future civilizations and their self-destruction.

Onscreen, the original *Matrix* film from 1999 remains one of the most gloriously energetic fantasies of virtual reality ever conceived; while the more recent film *Source Code* offers a more emotionally engaged – although still thrilling – exploration of virtual possibilities.

For mind-widening discussions of virtual worlds and much else besides online, the Terra Nova blog at terranova.blogs.com is the best place around for expert insights and debate.

If you want to experience complex virtual worlds for yourself, fine casual fun is to be had in games such as World of Warcraft – or more highly involved fun in EVE Online. Star Wars: The Old Republic also offers a gorgeously detailed digital environment to explore.

Free-to-play online games are best experienced through sites like Kongregate.com which gathers together thousands of amateur efforts and a vocal community of players.

8. The New Politics

For grasping the central human issues of contemporary politics, *Sovereign Virtue* by Ronald Dworkin (Harvard University Press, 2000) makes a radical case for putting equality at the heart of societies.

The great moral challenges of the twenty-first century have rarely been articulated more eloquently than by the philosopher Peter Singer in *The Life You Can Save* (Picador, 2009).

The most effective contemporary demolition of utopian aspirations surrounding digital technologies and politics is Evgeny Morozov's *The Net Delusion* (Allen Lane, 2011).

Another useful polemic is Eli Pariser's *The Filter Bubble* (Viking, 2011), which takes on the behind-the-scenes politics of data collection and customization.

Cory Doctorow's essay collection *Context* (Tachycon, 2011) offers a highly informed account of what the best digital activism can look like.

All digital students of human nature should find something to challenge established contexts via the economist Robin Hanson's blog Overcoming Bias at www.overcomingbias.com.

Conclusion

When it comes to what it means to live well in the present, Richard Holloway's *Godless Morality* (Canongate, 2004) remains a crisp, insightful starting point for getting down to ethical essentials.

Among the most philosophically literate technology books of recent years, *The Most Human Human* by Brian Christian (Viking,

2011) tells the story of the author's entry into an annual 'Turing test' designed to see if a machine can fool an interlocutor into thinking it is human.

You Are Not A Gadget by Jaron Lanier (Allen Lane, 2010) is a short, passionate manifesto about what technology and humanity should respectively mean.

One of fiction's greatest visions of the smallness of our understanding in the face of infinite possibilities remains Stanislaw Lem's 1961 novel *Solaris* (new edition Faber & Faber, 2003).

Another dizzying note on which to end is Greg Egan's science-fiction novel *Diaspora* (Gollancz, 2008) – a vision of universe-shifting technological futures.

Picture and Text Acknowledgements

The author and publisher would like to thank the following for permission to reproduce the images used in this book:

Page 5 Cloud Culture © Jeffrey Coolidge / Getty Images; Page 14–15 Hieroglyphics © De Agostini / Getty Images; Page 17 Milky Way © Design Pics Inc. / Alamy; Page 26–27 Dempsey vs. Carpentier © Corbis; Page 35 Blank clock © Aaron Foster / Getty Images; Page 41 Vase/face illusion © John Woodcock / iStockphoto; Page 45 Phrenology © World History Archive / Alamy; Page 51 My notebook © Antony Irvine 2011; Page 56–57 Silicon Valley © Ian Philip Miller / Getty Images; Page 63 Retinal scan © James King-Holmes / Science Photo Library; Page 71 Panthéon in Paris © Andrew Ward / Life File / Getty Images; Page 89 1920s erotic postcard © IBL Collections / Mary Evans Picture Library; Page 108–109 Internet cafe © Martin Puddy / Getty Images; Page 121 Occupy Seattle © Marilyn Dunstan Photography / Alamy; Page 125 CCTV © Gillian Blease / Getty Images; Page 136–137 School of Athens © SuperStock / Getty Images.

All other images provided courtesy of the author.

Every effort has been made to contact the copyright holders of the material reproduced in this book. If any have been inadvertently overlooked, the publisher will be pleased to make restitution at the earliest opportunity.

Page 3 extract is taken from Kevin Kelly's blog: www.kk.org/thetechnium/. Page 87 extract is taken from the foreword to *Crash*, J.G. Ballard (Jonathan Cape, 1973). Page 124 extract is taken from *The Net Delusion*, Evgeny Morozov (Perseus Books / Penguin / Brockman, 2011). Page 127 extract is taken from *The Master Switch*, Tim Wu (Random House US / Atlantic Books / Janklow and Nesbit, 2010). Page 47 is taken from *The Shallows*, Nicholas Carr (W.W. Norton & Co / Atlantic, 2011). Page extract 76 is taken from *Free Ride*, Robert Levine (Random House, 2011). Pages 138–139 extract is taken from *The Most Human Human*, Brian Christian (Random House/Viking UK, 2010).